GETTING TO GRIPS

By Toby Radford

FOREWORD:

Dawid Malan and Jason Holder

Published by New Generation Publishing in 2022

Copyright © Toby Radford 2022

First Edition

The author asserts the moral right under the Copyright, Designs and Patents Act 1988 to be identified as the author of this work.

All Rights reserved. No part of this publication may be reproduced, stored in a retrieval system or transmitted, in any form or by any means without the prior consent of the author, nor be otherwise circulated in any form of binding or cover other than that which it is published and without a similar condition being imposed on the subsequent purchaser.

ISBN
        Paperback   978-1-80369-331-6
        Ebook   978-1-80369-448-1

www.newgeneration-publishing.com

COVER:

Toby and Afif Dhrubo (Bangladesh)
Toby demo
Devon Conway (New Zealand)
Toby analysing a batsman's video footage

Acknowledgements

I should like to thank Sky and BT for allowing me to use the footage "screen grabs" for my technical analysis and all the players I have analysed here from the television footage, who will be helping to develop the next generation of players and coaches.

Some of the images have lost a little sharpness during the 'grab' and analysis process, but are still crisp enough for the relevant coaching message to be clearly conveyed.

On a personal note, I should like to thank Les Lenham, Bob Woolmer, John Harmer and Andy Wagner – all great coaches - whose time and knowledge helped my understanding of technique and movement patterns as I started out on my own coaching journey more than 25 years ago.

Huge thanks to my Mum and Dad for their unwavering love and support over the past 50 years.

Dad threw so many tennis balls at me when I was a young batter, that his right arm is now much longer than his left.

Mum made the packed lunches and always found a way to remove grass stains from my match-day whites.

To my beautiful wife Ayanna and ebullient 7-year-old son, Noah – so far, more of a runner than a cricketer – I thank them for their patience and understanding for the past two years when my eyes were often focused on my phone as I analysed yet another player, shot or set-up.

Thanks too, to Blank Bats and Richard Mansfield at Mansfield Sports Group MSG for supplying my coaching equipment and to my agents.

GETTING TO GRIPS

Contents

Foreword 1

Biography 4

When it all began … 5

Introduction 6

The Set-Up 9

Position at Ball Release....................................... 11

Pre-Delivery Movement (Trigger) 17

The Stance.. 21

The Grip 33

Guard and Alignment... 36

Right Hand Batsman Facing A Right Arm Over Bowler (Or Left Arm Around the wicket)… 37

Right Hand Batsman Facing A Left Arm Over Bowler (Or Right Arm Around Wicket) 56

Left Hand Batsman Facing Left Arm Over Bowler, (Or Right Arm Around Wicket)............................... 60

Left Hand Batsman Facing A Right Arm Over Bowler (Or Left Arm Around Wicket) 64

The Bat Tap / Pick up 68

The Backswing... 69

Moving To The Ball On The Front Foot … 79

Playing From A Stable Base On The Front Foot..... 86

From A Straight Line To A Straight Line................. 98

Moving To The Ball On The Back Foot … 101

- Playing From A Stable Base On The Back Foot ... 103
- The Square Cut 106
- The Pull Shot / Pivot-Pull 108
- Playing Against Deliveries That Angle Back Into The Stumps – Swing / Seam 112
- Playing Against Deliveries That Move Away From The Bat – Swing Or Seam 116
- Playing Swing – Playing Late 121
- Playing Spin – Advancing Down the Wicket 123
- Hitting Over The Top 126
- The Orthodox Sweep… 130
- The Slog Sweep … 132
- Power Hitting 137
- The "Helicopter Shot" 141
- The Batting Booth 143
- Other Photographs 159

FOREWORD

DAWID MALAN

England and Yorkshire batsman

Toby Radford has played an important role in my development as a cricketer.

As Middlesex coach in 2007, 2008 and 2009, he offered excellent technical advice and, crucially, instilled in me a strong work ethic. In fact, in my entire career, I have never known a coach to work so hard improving his players' techniques.

His commitment to wanting players to improve really stood out and he knew what he was talking about; specifically, I remember how he raised some issues with my trigger movement. I listened, made the changes he suggested, and improved as a result of implementing these changes.

I am pleased Toby has put his thoughts and views on technique down on paper, for a wider audience to enjoy.

SHIVNARINE CHANDERPAUL

West Indies international, and former world number-one Test batsman

As a player, I was always keen to work hard on my game and to keep developing. Always looking for that little bit extra. Never satisfied.

I worked closely with Toby when he came in as batting coach for the West Indies team. We talked through my daily practice routine using the bowling machine. Connect with the ball close to his head. I would do it to keep my judgment in good shape and to know what deliveries to play around off-stump, and the ones not to play.

Toby and I always got on well together. We spoke the same technical language and had a similar high work ethic.

As we trained more together, Toby would go through the various drills and routines and would feed back to me about my balance and head position: I always knew that if these were good that I was where I wanted to be to perform in the middle.

I love the simplicity of this book and how Toby manages to communicate quite complex technical information in such an innovative way - with clever images, diagrams and notes - that the message is conveyed with absolute clarity.

This book combines Toby's two main strengths - technical batting knowledge and communication skills.

Players and coaches at all levels of ability will benefit hugely from this book. Their understanding of batting and the movement patterns involved with it - so simply shown and put - will grow enormously.

Shiv

JASON HOLDER

West Indies world number-one Test Match all-rounder

I first met 'Radders' in my stint at what was then the Sagicor High Performance Centre in Barbados, where I was transformed into the professional athlete that I am today.

Toby made my batting a lot tighter, and more aligned, to be successful at the highest level.

His key points were alignment and head position, which gave me the best access to any delivery that I could encounter.

We spent many hours working on my unique bat path where my hands drop just at ball-release, and my shoulders open up. This means my bat can come from point or gully to line up with the ball.

Thanks to lots of hard work and discussion, we made the movement consistent and created a game plan around it. It became effective for me.

This book will provide ideal batting set-up positions and show how to move effectively and efficiently to play the strokes.

Toby and I worked really well together. We put in many hours of practice to achieve our targets. But we never forgot the most important component of them all - to have FUN! We enjoyed the hard work and made sure we did it with a smile on our face.

Do enjoy every minute that you play our great game, and I am sure this book will give you a much better understanding of the vital basics of batting.

Jase.

Biography

TOBY Radford is widely regarded as one of the best batting coaches in the game.

Toby was head coach when Middlesex were crowned English T20 champions in 2008, and batting coach when the West Indies won the T20 world cup in Sri Lanka in 2012.

Following a successful spell as an England & Wales (ECB) national coach, Toby launched the Middlesex Academy, which produced England Test stars Steven Finn, Eoin Morgan, and Dawid Malan.

In 2010, Toby set up the West Indies High Performance Centre in Barbados, from where seven of his impressive students graduated to the senior Test team, led by the towering Jason Holder, who went on to become world number-one all-rounder.

After ten enjoyable years of coaching in the Caribbean, and working with greats of the game such as Shiv Chanderpaul, Chris Gayle and Marlon Samuels, Toby has been Head of Performance for Bangladesh Cricket, working with, among others, Afif Dhrubo and Mahmudul Hassan Joy, who have gone on to perform so well for the senior international side.

Toby was thrilled in February to help England Young Lions reach their first world cup final for 25 years.

Passionate about developing the coaches of the future, Toby has written and delivered a number of batting modules for the ECB's advanced coaching programme and also mentors several coaches for the game's governing body.

WHEN it all began ... Toby immaculately dressed to launch his cricket career in mid-June 1977. He was four. Father, Brian, peeps through the stumps.

Introduction

During my role as batting coach with the West Indies team, there were often periods between international series when I would return home to the UK and the players to their respective Caribbean islands.

To maintain contact and ensure that their game was kept in good working order, they would send me footage from their practices and net sessions.

I would study the footage and then highlight screen grabs with relevant text and drawings for attention and work. These would be sent and received via WhatsApp on a mobile phone.

Feedback from the West Indian batsmen was very positive. They said they liked the visual notes and the clarity and immediacy of the feedback.

They would work on the areas we highlighted and discussed and send further footage through for me to monitor the improvement.

When the Covid pandemic hit in early 2020, so many players of all ages, abilities and gender were unable to practice, play matches and access coaching sessions.

It dawned on me that offering the same service to the general cricket playing public that Test players had been enjoying and benefiting from, could help those players who were keen to work on their game, but frustratingly confined to their home.

I added a section to my existing batting coaching website, where players could register and then send me via WhatsApp their own batting footage for me to assess.

Within weeks, I was receiving footage from across the world. From India, Australia, the Caribbean; club cricketers, academy players and international batsmen alike. It gave me immense satisfaction to be able to offer in-depth analysis and simple solutions to a variety of batsmen around the globe.

I always aimed to return my observational notes to players as quickly as possible and with the wonders of technology - mobile phone camera development and the immediacy of the WhatsApp messaging service – I was able at one point to give feedback to a batsman in Australia, from my home thousands of miles away in Cardiff, while he was still in the net! It was instantaneous. I felt as though I was actually there coaching him.

Throughout the pandemic, I have continued to analyse, make recommendations and offer technical and tactical solutions to players sending me their footage to the Batting Booth.

During the year, I have also made many Instagram posts highlighting the techniques of the world's best batsmen. What it is that makes them so effective and world's best. Those often simple things that make such a difference to performance - like head position, body alignment, keeping the hands and bat close to the body; the fundamentals of batting that help top batsmen deliver within the broader parameter of having their own shots, flair and individuality.

By highlighting the key fundamentals, I am hoping to help players of all ages and abilities to improve their game.

Many coaches have contacted me and said how they have enjoyed the Instagram posts and are using observations from them in their own coaching work.

I hope that this book, which is very visual in nature, will offer some insight, new ideas and practical solutions to common batting problems. If you are a player or a coach, hopefully it will help you in your search for success.

It is not an a to z of coaching or a definitive coaching encyclopedia. More what I have learned and experienced during my time as an international batting coach and my findings from observing close-up and personal the world's best batsmen as they practiced and performed in a variety of conditions.

A huge thanks to all the players of differing levels and abilities who feature in this book for helping us to continue our learning about the wonderful art of batting

I hope you enjoy the read.

The Set-Up

HOW a batsman sets up, and especially his or her position at ball release is crucial. So many batting issues arise from a set-up that hinders effective movement and a consistent bat path to the ball.

The shots themselves are not difficult to play, but they are if players are unable to move quickly into the appropriate, balanced position to play them.

It is important that coaches acknowledge and accept individual differences between players. No two players play the same way and neither should they. Individuality and flair are what makes sport compelling viewing. Virat Kohli's poetic cover drive, Viv Richard's trademark flick over square leg or Robin Smith's blistering square cuts.

Dig a little deeper beneath the glossy exterior of these fine players and other world class batsmen and what do we find?

Whether it is Steve Smith, Babar Azam, Kane Williamson, Ben Stokes or Marnus Labuschagne, each has his 'go to' shots, favours scoring in slightly different parts of the field, their individuality.

They also meet five key fundamentals which form the basis and the technical foundation of their batting.

Flashy alloys and glistening paint are only added to a Ferrari once the strong chassis is in place.

Batting is no different. Flair and funk are only added when a solid technical foundation and the key fundamentals are in place.

The FIVE key fundamentals;

1. The head is close to off-stump / middle and off-stump at ball release.

2. The hands and bat are kept close to the body at ball release and the top hand dominates the backswing and bat path.

3. The head and body align towards the bowler's stumps at ball release (RH bat v RH bowler) and the body is in a dynamic position (knees slightly bent) to enable quick movement forward or back.

4. The batsman tracks the ball in early flight and moves to the finishing line.

5. Contact with the ball is made close to the body (near the head) and from a stable base.

Position at Ball Release

The head is close to off-stump / middle and off-stump at ball release

SOME batsmen prefer to stand still at release, while others will get there following a 'trigger' or pre-delivery movement, which gets their feet and body ready to spring into action.

Whatever movement comes before the position at ball release is very much a personal choice.

It is crucial though, that the position at ball release enables quick movement forward and back and easy access to all lines of delivery.

The current trend with the world's best batsmen (RH bat v RH bowl or LH bat v LH bowl) is to position their head close to off-stump at ball release.

This helps them to judge more easily whether to play or leave deliveries pitching in and around the off-stump channel.

Against real pace, anything outside the eye line can be left, and the feet and body are already in position for those directed straighter.

With the head and back foot already close to the off-stump channel – the "business area" where most top bowlers bowl – crucial time is saved from moving across the crease to get into line against deliveries travelling at speeds of up to 95 mph at the top end of the game.

Steve Smith and Marnus Labuschagne were highly successful using this method against the pace of Jofra Archer in the 2019 Ashes Series.

Between them, they amassed 1127 runs, which included 3 hundreds and 7 fifties. Smith struck 774 runs at an average of 110.57 and Labuschagne 353 in that series at an average of 50.

Pakistan's Babar Azam currently averages 42.5 in Test matches, 56 in one-day internationals. Until recently he was rated number-one T20 player in the world. Ben Stokes, another who positions his head at off-stump at ball release, averages 37 in Tests and 40 in ODI's.

The top players make subtle adjustments to this positioning based on the conditions they play in and the bowlers they face. They bring their guard back a little so that their head finishes closer to middle stump at ball release when coping with excess and late lateral movement (especially in conditions similar to those often witnessed early season in the county championship in England, where quality bowling on damp, green pitches with a proud-seamed Dukes ball make batsmen battle hard for every run).

Position at Ball Release

Many of the world's best batsmen – Babar Azam, Steve Smith, Ben Stokes, AB de Villiers, Marnus Labuschagne, Darren Stevens etc… have their head close to off-stump at ball release and align their body to the bowler's stumps so that they can judge off-stump easily and access all lines of delivery.

They "open" their front foot slightly and focus on their head staying forward and NOT drifting outside off-stump when the ball is released. This helps them to play straight to any deliveries that swing, seam or angle back at the stumps.

Position at Ball Release

Babar Azam (Pakistan)

Babar Azam – ranked number one batsman in the world in ODI's, third in T20 and tenth in Test Cricket.

The Pakistan captain has a wonderful position at ball release.

- Head close to off-stump
- Hands close to his body and under his head
- Head and shoulders face the bowler's stumps
- Feet slightly open to help access all lines of delivery

Position at Ball Release

Marnus Labuschagne (Australia and Glamorgan CCC)

Ranked third highest in the world, Marnus Labuschagne, is another top class batsman who has his head close to off-stump at ball release.

He is seen above during his innings of 77 for Glamorgan against Northamptonshire in Cardiff.

His head is still, hands are under his head and he creates an imaginary straight line from his head through his hands to his feet for wonderful balance and easier control of the bat.

Position at Ball Release

Tom Cullen (Glamorgan CCC)

Glamorgan batsman Tom Cullen working hard to get his head, hands and feet to line up to improve his balance and ease of movement.

Pre-Delivery Movement (Trigger)

Most international batsmen have some form of movement prior to ball release to fire up the muscles and get the feet ready to access all lines and differing lengths of delivery

Tennis players adopt a similar movement – a shuffling of their feet and bodyweight when looking to return fast serves.

The timing of a trigger is important. If it is late – just at, or after, ball release – the player is often rushed to get into position. Balance and stability are not created at contact so control and power are lost in the shot.

If a trigger is too early – well before ball release – the benefit of it 'firing up the system' to move, is lost.

Ideally, any movement should be made just as the pace bowler bounds (jumps) and takes the ball up in his gather.

There are many different types of trigger. Some players feel comfortable with a forward press, others take their back foot towards off-stump, while many like to move both feet, either forward or back.

Whatever movement a batsman adopts, it needs to be comfortable, consistent and effective. If the movement does not create a balanced position for good judgment at ball release and enable quick and easy movement forward and back, to all lines of delivery, then it is not an effective trigger. It is a batting hindrance, not a help.

I appreciate and welcome a player's personal preferences with his movements but I have found the most successful players tend to have smaller movements (less to go wrong), move earlier rather than later (not then rushed), maintain a steady head position at ball release and are well aligned to move up and down the wicket and access all lines of delivery easily.

Common Problems ...

- ❖ Move too early and lose the benefit
- ❖ Move too late and rush the stroke – never balanced or in control
- ❖ Not aligned well at ball release – hips, feet and shoulders not facing towards bowler's stumps
- ❖ Weight on back leg at release – takes longer to get onto the front foot
- ❖ Head outside line of feet at release – weight moves early to the off side which can lead to playing across straighter deliveries

Practise the Trigger...

- In the mirror
- Film it in practice to see if the movement is effective and consistent
- Make two marks on the ground – the guard to start from and a mark to end up on after the trigger movement. Check in practice that you hit the position (chalk indoors / make mark on grass in outdoor net / middle
- Start with underarm bobble feed drills – make sure trigger is complete before ball is fed.
- Increase pace of feeds and when movement is consistent, progress the drill to overarm throws / flings / bowling

The Trigger

The world's top ICC ranked batsmen – Joe Root, Marnus Labuschagne, Steve Smith, Rohit Sharma and Kane Williamson – all have a subtle "trigger" or pre-delivery movement prior to release of the ball.

An effective trigger helps them to move forward and back quickly into the appropriate position to play the shot.

They make their trigger early and, in most cases, it is a small and subtle movement.

After the trigger, their…

- Head is still for accurate judgment of line and length

- Their face and body align towards the bowler's stumps for easy access to all lines of delivery

- Head and bodyweight are slightly forward to enable quick movement onto the front foot and the transfer of weight against it when looking to move back to play shorter deliveries.

The Stance

Head – slightly forward and eyes parallel with the ground. Creating an imaginary straight line from the head, through the hands and into the feet (or close to them) enables quick and easy movement forward and back.

Shoulders – relaxed and slightly "open" to allow the head to come forward. Front shoulder dipped forward to help bring head and bodyweight forward and closer to the front foot. This helps for quicker movement forward onto the front foot and a press off the front foot to transfer weight quickly when playing back.

Front elbow, top hand and front shoulder create a straight line towards the bowler's stumps.

Hips – slightly "open" and aligned to the bowler's stumps.

Knees – a slight flex. A dynamic position, ready for fast movement forward or back.

Feet - a comfortable distance apart (often shoulder width). Front foot is positioned just inside the line of the back foot to enable easy access to straighter deliveries and also to help bodyweight to align back at the bowler's stumps. Many players have their front foot pointing towards extra cover to help direct their bodyweight down the wicket rather than across it. Having slightly more weight over the front foot enables quick weight transfer and movement in both directions.

Practice drills for set-up

* In the mirror
* Film it
* Close eyes and, when open, see if body position is as desired

The Stance

Ollie Pope   **A B de Villiers**

Head and body align to the bowler's stumps to allow easy movement forward and back and access to all lines of delivery.

The Stance

Balance at Ball Release....

West Indies batting stars Lendl Simmons (left) and Nicholas Pooran are well positioned to move easily and efficiently here at ball release.

Having the head close to the front foot at release helps quick movement either froward or back and keeping the hands close to, and at the middle of the body, keeps the weight forward and encourages the front shoulder and top hand to control the bat

The Stance

Janneman Malan (South Africa)

I love this position!

- Head is close to the front foot to enable easy movement forward and back
- The hands and bat are close to the body (at the midriff) for control
- The shoulders and feet are slightly open to enable the head and body to access all lines of delivery easily.

The Stance

Two different South African batsmen (Janneman Malan and A B de Villiers) but the same position at ball release shown here from front and side on.

- Head is close to the front foot to enable easy movement forward and back
- The hands and bat are close to the body (at the midriff) for control
- The shoulders and feet are slightly open to enable the head and body to access all lines of delivery easily.

Creating good balance at ball release!
Ideally have slightly more weight over the front foot to enable quick movement both forward and back.

Photo on right …
Look to create…
* a bend of both knees to be dynamic and ready to move (no bend creates static position)
* the front knee to bend forward to bring weight forward (not bend sideways)
* the head to be close to or over the front foot (but not beyond it)
* front elbow bends to bring weight forward

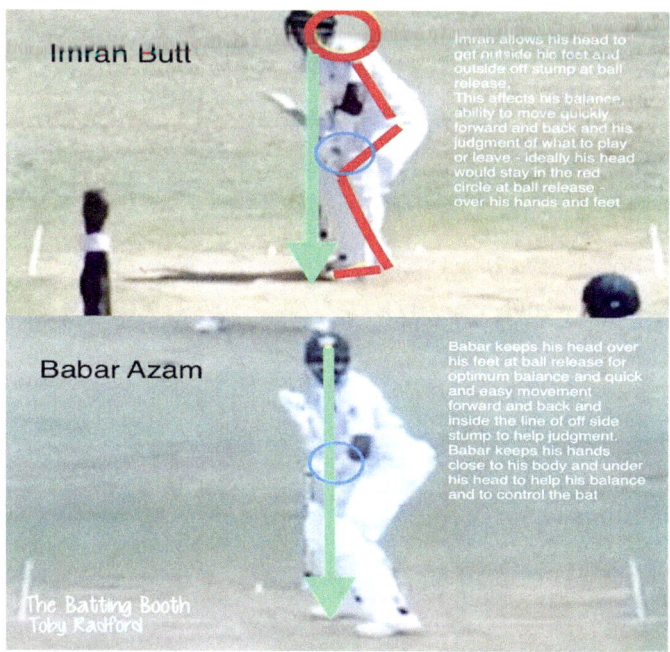

PAKISTAN opener Imran Butt allows his head to drift well outside his feet, and outside off-stump at ball release, which affects his balance, and his ability to move quickly and easily to the correct position for the shot.

Ideally, his head should remain inside the red circle at ball release, above his hands and his feet.

In contrast, Butt's colleague, Babar Azam, has kept his head over his feet, and inside the line of off-stump for quick movement forward and back.

It also places him in a good position to judge what to play and what to leave, as well as optimum control of the bat.

Feroze Khushi (Essex)

Young Essex batsman Feroze Khushi worked hard to improve his balance at ball release. He straightened his back slightly, bent his knees more, and looked to create an imaginary straight line from his head, through his hands to his feet.

He had a great season in 2020 and was named ESSEX CCC Young Player of the Year. It was great to see all his hard work paying off.

Kyle Corbin (Barbados)

Bringing his head forward further (into black circle) will put slightly more weight on his front foot to aid quicker movement forward and back.

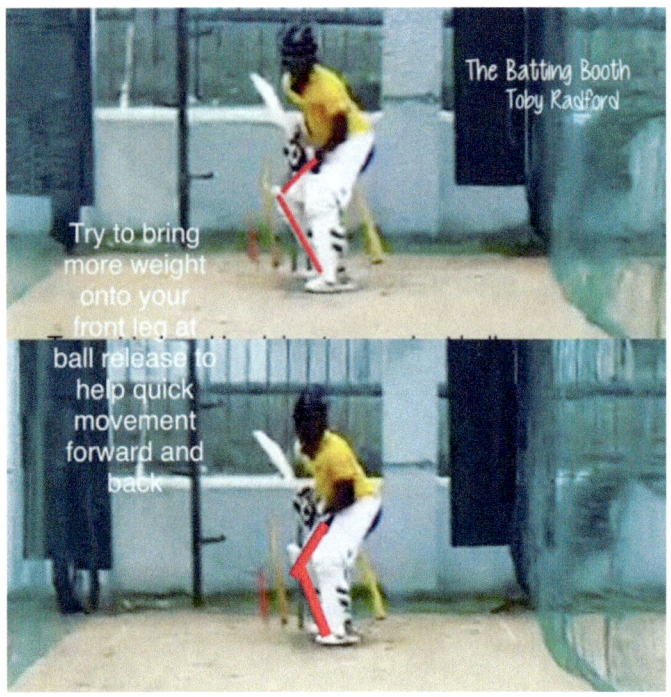

Kevin Stoute (Windward Islands)

Too much bend on Kevin's back leg at ball release is affecting his ability to get quickly onto the front foot when required.

Once the weight gets over his front foot at ball release, he will be able to move forward much quicker.

Joe Cooke (Glamorgan CCC)

With so much weight on Joe's collapsed back leg at ball release (red line) it is very difficult for him to transfer his weight, and to get his head and front foot close to full deliveries.

This delivery bowls him because his front foot does not move from its position in his stance (blue circle).

For Joe to get into top form, he would benefit from…

- Dipping his shoulders and head forward at ball release (they are tipped backwards presently)

- Having more bodyweight over his front leg. With less bodyweight over his bent back knee.

Zak Crawley (England and Kent CCC)

It was good to see Zak Crawley improving his alignment and weight distribution at ball release after a run of disappointing scores.

The adjustments Zak made were…

- Less bend of, and weight on, his back leg
- His head is now inside the line of off-stump (yellow arrow)
- His top hand and front elbow now align towards the bowler's stumps (green arrow)

His front shoulder is almost too sideways and might make accessing leg stump deliveries a little awkward. Ideally, the front shoulder should be slightly open and align towards the bowler's stumps

The Grip

The grip is very personal. It needs to be comfortable and also effective. The top hand and front shoulder should control the backswing and the bat path.

The top hand grip – fingers underneath the handle, a strong grip, with the wrist firm and a position which enables a straight line to run from the top hand, through the elbow to the bowler's stumps. This alignment helps to bring the bat down in a straight line. Modern players tend to have the "v" between thumb and finger on the top hand running down the middle of the handle.

The bottom hand – a softer grip, with the 'v' between the thumb and finger of the bottom hand running down the outside splice at the bottom of handle. The bottom hand supports and adds power into shots, but comes behind the front hand. Very rarely does it dominate the stroke.

Ideally, the two hands will work together on the handle and be positioned close together.

Getting the correct grip

- Mark the position for the top and bottom hand "v's" in black pen. This ensures a consistent grip

- Make the bottom of the handle slightly thicker – by placing tape underneath – to encourage a looser bottom hand grip to enable the top hand to dominate the backswing and bat path.

- Hit front foot drives from bobble feed with only the top hand holding the bat. To control the ball, the shoulders have to rotate vertically and the top hand, wrist and forearm remain firm at contact. The head will need to be over the front knee at ball contact, which should be made from a stable base.

Players often adjust their top hand grip during the drill to give them a cleaner strike (middle of the bat and a crisp sound as the ball leaves it), and more consistent control of the bat face.

As strike consistently improves, the bottom hand can be added to the handle while the bat is at full extension during the drive. By placing the bottom hand at full reach, it encourages a less dominant bottom hand grip. Many players find their bottom hand positions itself in a subtly different place on the handle.

Progression of this drill, which works so well for improving many issues (grip, weight transfer onto the front foot, bat path, head position and balance etc) works well when the player alternates from top hand, both hands, back to top hand.

When strike becomes very clean and consistent, all shots can be played with both hands on the handle.

Very often, players find that they have very subtly altered the positioning of one or both of their hands to get them working well together and for the top hand to dominate the backswing and bat path effectively.

Amari Ebbin (Bermuda) – demonstrating the Top Hand Front Foot Drill

Guard and Alignment

The guard that players take and how they align their body (feet, hips and shoulders) in the set-up and at ball release is crucial as this determines how easily they can move to the ball and present a full face of the bat to the ball.

Many professional batsmen adopt a different guard and alignment when facing bowlers from over and around the wicket.

A right handed batsman facing a right arm over bowler (same for left handed batsman facing left arm over bowler), often positions his head close to off-stump at ball release and aligns the body towards the bowler's stumps.

When he faces a left arm over bowler (left handed batsman facing right arm over bowler), the head is over middle stump at ball release and the body aligns to the bowler's hand. This helps to cope with late in-swing which is so often the major threat from that angle of delivery.

Right hand batsman facing a right arm over bowler (or left arm around)…

- Head at ball release…

Many top international batsmen adopt a position where their head is close to **off-stump** at ball release for them to be near the line that most bowlers bowl. Against quicker bowling, having the head close to off-stump reduces the amount of foot movement required to get into position to play the shot and it becomes easier to judge what to play and what to leave.

Pakistan's Babar Azam, Australia's Steve Smith and Marnus Labuschagne, and New Zealander Kane Williamson are just a few world class right-handed batsmen who adopt this off-stump head position at ball release.

The head and front shoulder dip slightly forward towards the bowler's stumps.

- Shoulder, hip and feet alignment …

Slightly 'open' at ball release. This helps the weight to go back towards the bowler's stumps (remains neutral) and with the front leg and foot slightly open it makes for easier access to deliveries angling back into the stumps.

- Hands and bat….

The hands and bat are kept close to the body (under the head) and close to the midriff to maintain good balance, control and for generating more power. The top hand and front elbow align to the bowler's stumps. The toe of the bat points upwards (unweighting) for a longer and more rhythmical swing and for easier control and to come down on top of shorter, bouncing deliveries. The bat is visible to the bowler throughout.

- Straight line from head, through hands to feet…

Creating an imaginary straight line from the head, through the hands to the feet at ball release, enables easy movement forward and back to all lines of delivery and optimum control of the bat.

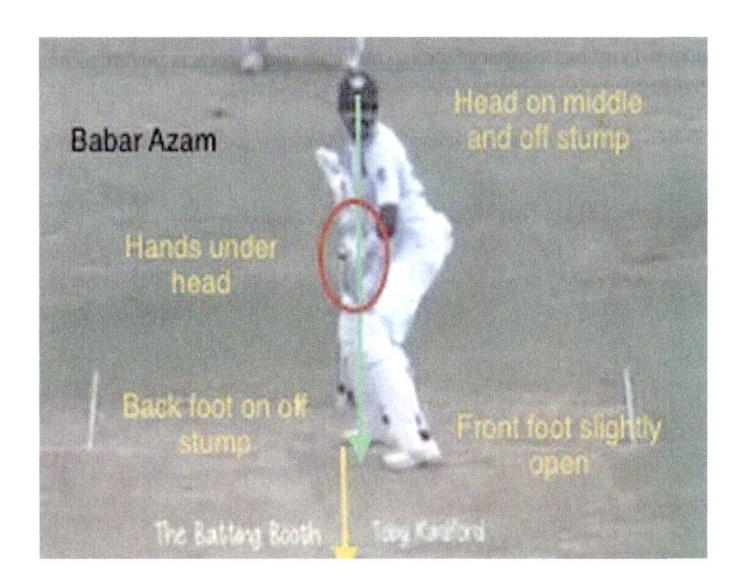

Babar Azam (Pakistan)

Babar stands with back toe in front of off-stump at ball release.

His hands and bat stay close to his body and under his head with the toe of the bat always visible to the bowler (to help him access all lines of delivery)

His head and shoulders face the bowler's stumps and his front foot is slightly open to help his balance and to give him easier access to straighter and leg stump deliveries.

Babar is world class in all formats of the game.

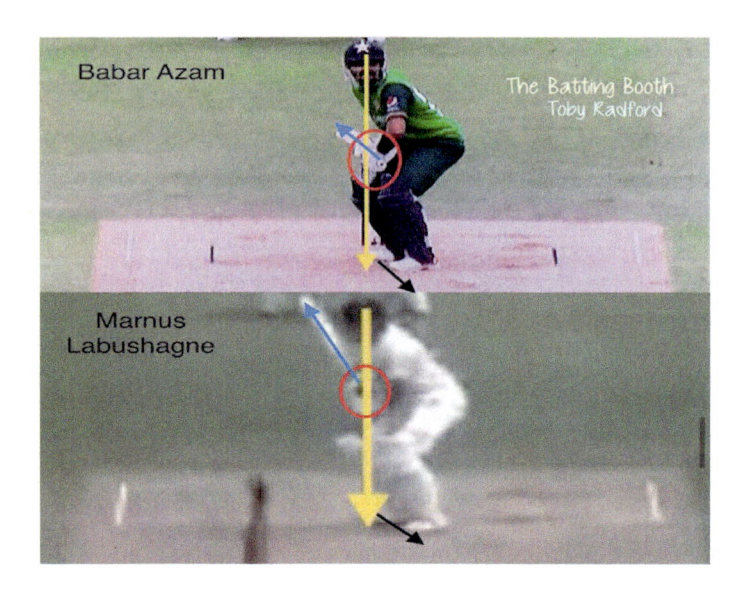

World-class batsmen, Babar Azam and Marnus Labuschagne, world number three, have virtually the same position at ball release.

Both of them have their:

- Head close to off-stump
- Head and front shoulder forward
- Hands close to the body and under the head
- Shoulders slightly 'open'
- Feet slightly 'open'
- Knees bent to allow quick movement forward and back
- Face and body towards the bowler's stumps
- Toe of bat visible to bowler

A B de Villiers (South Africa)

A B de Villiers is wonderfully balanced. From his position at ball release, he can move quickly forward and back and access all lines of delivery. He is watching the ball in the bowler's hand but has his face aligned towards the bowler's stumps.

Rohit Sharma (India)

Rohit Sharma aligns himself to the bowler's stumps and keeps his hands close to his body and under his head at ball release. He is well positioned to be able to move quickly in all directions

Good position at release - head on off stump and head and front shoulder (bodyweight) towards bowler's stumps

Saif Hassan (Bangladesh)

Bangladesh batsman, Saif Hassan, has opened his front foot and front shoulder slightly to bring his head and body weight more towards the bowler's stumps at ball release. This helps him to access all lines of delivery.

Ross Taylor (New Zealand)

Ross Taylor displays superb technique and alignment at ball release. His head is close to being above off-stump, his hands are tight to his body, and his feet are aligned to the bowler's stumps.

Darren Stevens (Kent CCC)

Beautiful balance at ball release from Kent's Darren Stevens. His hands are under his head and weight is wonderfully distributed

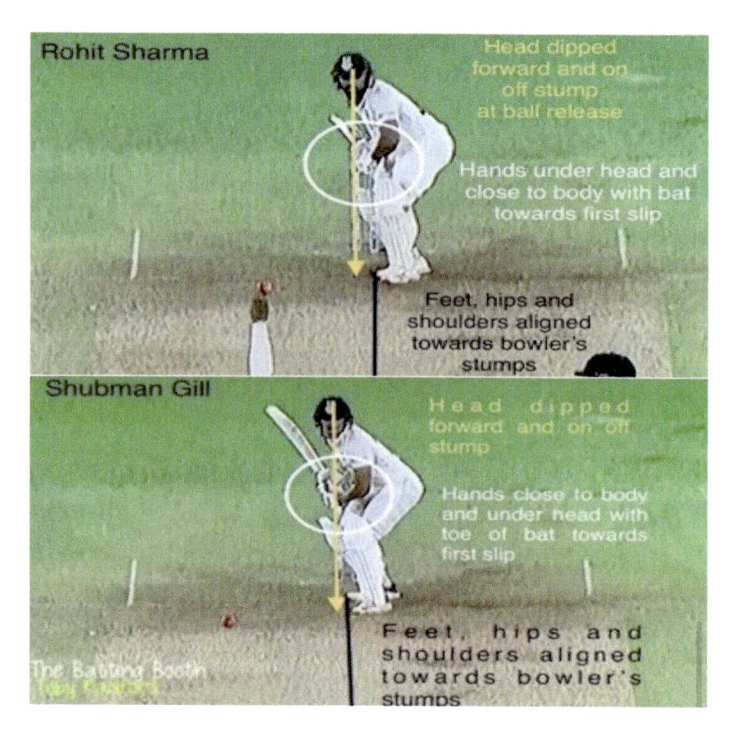

Rohit Sharma and Shubman Gill (india)

India's two top openers display excellent balance and alignment at ball release which helps them move quickly and efficiently to the ball.

- Head is close to off-stump and the "business area"
- Feet, shoulders and hips align towards the bowler's stumps for ease of movement up and down the wicket
- Hands are kept close to the body and under the head, with the toe of the bat towards first slip, to help with control of the bat and its presentation to all lines of delivery.

A leg-stump guard often encourages a batsman to move his/her head across to the off-side to meet the line of the ball.

Once the head goes outside the line of the feet, balance is affected, and it becomes very difficult to get into the appropriate position for the shot.

Guard (Joshua Bishop Barbados)

The guard you take can have a huge impact on balance and ability to access lines of delivery easily.

Barbados batsman, Joshua Bishop, is affected here by a leg-stump guard, which forces his head across, rather than down the wicket.

An earlier trigger movement, with his head and back foot closer to off-stump at ball-release would make accessing all lines of delivery much easier for him.

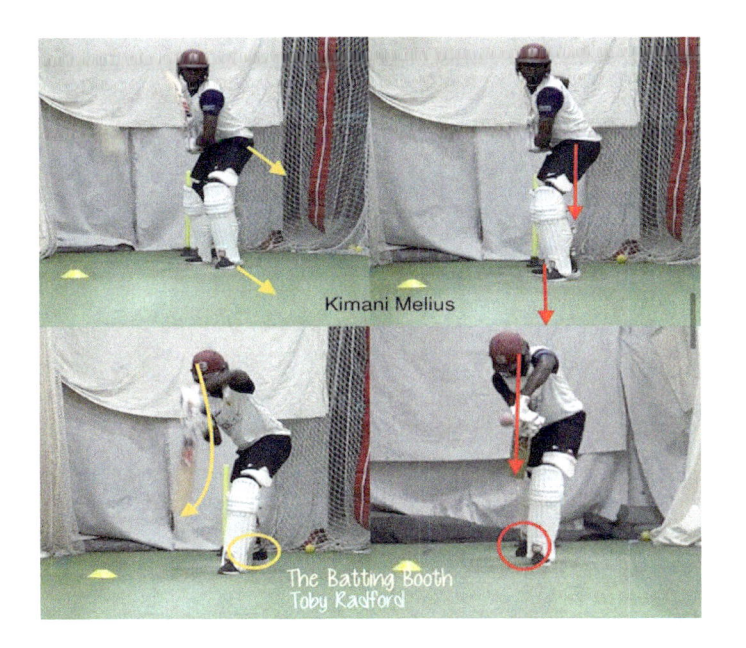

Kimani Melius (Windward Islands)

Kimani's very open front hip and front foot (yellow lines) has made it difficult for him to move his head forward and close to the ball to judge confidently and play away-swingers deliveries in and around the off-stump channel.

His judgment in the channel was inconsistent and, when he decided to play, many deliveries ran square or behind the wicket off the outer half of the bat. The heel of his back foot (yellow circle) was often on the floor at contact, which was keeping his weight back in the shot and his head well behind his front foot at ball contact. Kimani was connecting with the ball early and a long way in front of his head and body.

By aligning his feet, hips and shoulders (red lines) to the bowler's stumps at ball release, Kimani was able to bring his head and front shoulder further forward in the set-up and then move it closer to the finishing line of the ball.

Kimani started to connect with the ball while having his head over his front foot which gave him more control, better timing and increased power. The heel of his back foot started to come off the floor (red circle), which also helped to bring his head further forward.

The subtle changes enabled Kimani to present a much fuller bat face at the ball and to play a lot straighter.

Kimani Melius (Windward Islands)

WE spent a lot of time working on Kimani's alignment. When we began, his shoulders were facing mid-off at ball-release, which forced his bat to come across his body, and slightly across the line of the ball. He was rotating on shots.

Once he opened his front shoulder, and the toe of the bat became visible, he could get closer to the ball on the front foot (stay side-on) and create a straight bat path to the ball.

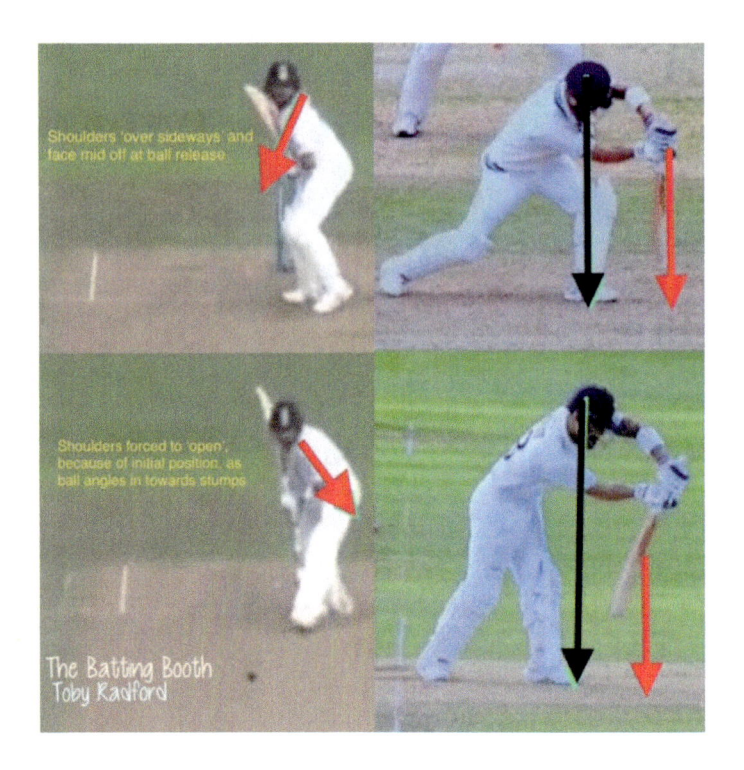

Virat Kohli (India)

The side-on images of his dismissals (right) show just how far in front of his body his bat was connecting with the ball. Ideally, contact is made under his head for optimum control, timing, and power.

Virat's shoulders are over-sideways at ball-release (facing mid-off), which keeps his head and body weight slightly back, and to the off-side. His shoulders are then forced to open as deliveries angle back towards the stumps.

When deliveries then swing late in the other direction the bat is forced to come down across the line of the ball.

Virat will find it easier to play the late away-swinger in difficult English conditions if…

1. He opens his front shoulder slightly at ball-release and aligns it to the bowler's stumps. This will help his head to come forward for better judgment and weight transfer to help him access all lines of delivery without having to open his front shoulder on the shot.

2. Allow the ball to swing, and then look to connect with it close to his body and under his head

Subtle changes….

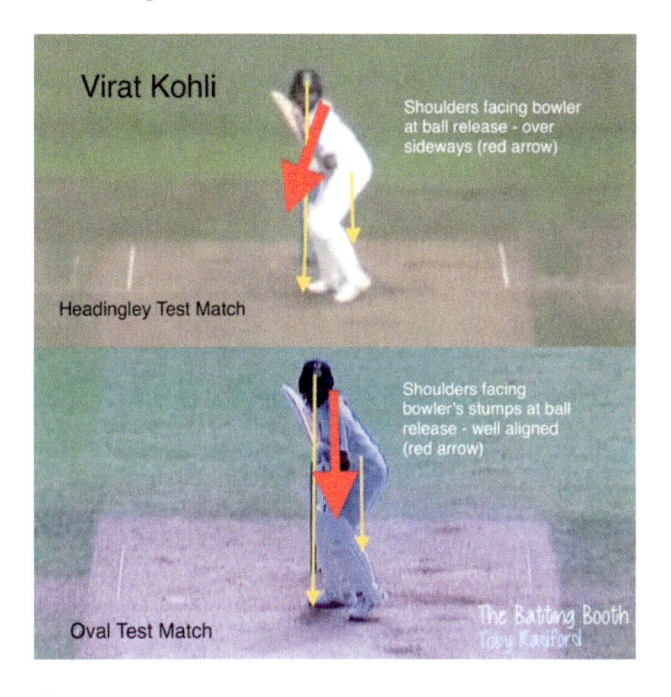

Virat Kohli (India)
Virat Kohli made subtle changes to his set-up during a Test match against England at the Oval in 2021.

He opened his front shoulder (red arrow), which had been over-sideways in previous innings, causing him to face mid-off at ball-release.

Kohli consequently played more fluently, and scored 50 in his first innings, and 44 when he batted second time.

He was now aligning his shoulders to the bowler's stumps at ball-release, which enabled him to bring his head and weight further forward and, therefore, transfer his weight quicker onto the front foot.

Kohli, like Rohit Sharma, Babar Azam, Steve Smith, and many other top international batsmen, has his head close to off-stump at ball-release, his hands under his head, and he aligns his hips to the bowler's stumps.

Haseeb Hameed (England, Nottinghamshire CCC) and Babar Azam (Pakistan)

Haseeb has his shoulders and face pointing towards the bowler, which then affects his ability to move easily and to access all lines of delivery. In contrast, Babar Azam has his face and shoulders aligned to the bowler's stumps to enable quick movement up and down the wicket and easier access to all lines of delivery.

Right-hand batsman facing a left-arm over-the-wicket bowler or right-arm bowler coming from around the wicket

- Head at ball release...

The head is over **middle stump** at ball release and it faces the bowler's hand. This helps for coping with the late in-swing, so often the major threat from this angle of delivery.

- Shoulder, hip and feet alignment ...

The feet, hips and shoulders align towards the bowler's hand. The front leg and foot are slightly open for easier access to deliveries swinging back in towards the stumps.

- Hands and bat....

The hands and bat are kept close to the body (under the head) and close to the midriff to maintain good balance, control and for generating more power. The top hand and front elbow align to the bowler. The toe of the bat points upwards (unweighting) for a longer and more rhythmical swing and for easier control and to come down on top of shorter, bouncing deliveries. The bat is visible to the bowler throughout.

- Straight line from head, through hands to feet...

Creating an imaginary straight line from the head, through the hands to the feet at ball release, enables easy movement forward and back, to all lines of delivery and optimum control of the bat.

Feroze Khushi (Essex CCC)

WHEN facing left-arm swing, WAIT as long as possible to allow the ball to swing, and then meet the finishing line of the ball.

These images show an early commitment to play on the off-side. The shoulders align towards mid-off, the bat is then behind his head. He is forced to play across the line of the ball and the ball sneaks through the gap to bowl him.

> Head wants to be on middle in yellow circle for an jnswjng left armer. It's outside off stump here. Easy to adjust your guard for the left armer to achieve this

Saif Hassan (Bangladesh)

SAIF Hassan's head needs to be over middle-stump (yellow circle) for a left-arm seamer's in-swinger.

This time, his head is outside the off-stump, so he needs to adjust his guard for a left-arm seamer.

George Bell (Lancashire CCC and England Under 19)

George's head just dips across a little to the off-stump at ball release which makes him vulnerable when the ball then swings back from the left-arm seamer.

We discussed and worked on keeping the head over middle, middle-and-leg stump and facing towards the bowler's hand. This helps him to access all lines of delivery and to be able to hit straight when the ball swings back in at him.

Left-hand batsman facing left-arm-over bowler, or right-arm around the wicket

- Head at ball release…

England's Ben Stokes and New Zealand's Devon Conway, are two top left handers who adopt the off-stump head position at ball release. The head and front shoulder also dip slightly forward towards the bowler's stumps

- Shoulder, hip and feet alignment …

Slightly 'open' at ball release. This helps the weight to go back towards the bowler's stumps (remains neutral) and with the front leg and foot slightly open it makes for easier access to deliveries angling back into the stumps.

- Hands and bat….

The hands and bat are kept close to the body (under the head) and close to the midriff to maintain good balance, control and for generating more power. The top hand and front elbow align to the bowler's stumps. The toe of the bat points upwards (unweighting) for a longer and more rhythmical swing and for easier control and to come down on top of shorter, bouncing deliveries. The bat is visible to the bowler throughout.

- Straight line from head, through hands to feet…

Creating an imaginary straight line from the head, through the hands to the feet at ball release, enables easy movement forward and back, to all lines of delivery and optimum control of the bat.

Devon Conway (New Zealand)

Devon Conway has his head and back foot close to off-stump at ball release when facing bowlers from around the wicket, to be close to the off-stump channel. His hips, feet and shoulders are slightly open and he faces the bowler's stumps to enable easy access to straighter deliveries

Subtle Changes

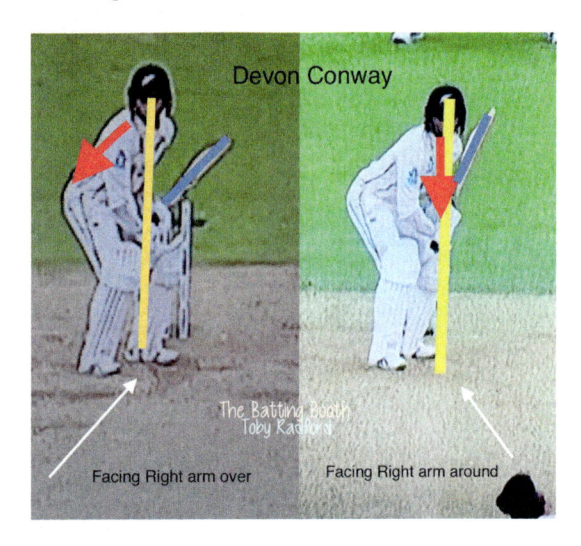

Devon Conway (New Zealand)

Like most world class batsmen, New Zealand's Devon Conway makes subtle changes to his guard and alignment when facing bowling from over and around the wicket.

Facing from over the wicket his head is over middle-and-leg stump guard for easier access to in-swinging and straighter deliveries, and he faces the bowler. The toe of his bat is taken slightly wider towards third slip to help him present a straight bat path and full bat face to the angle of delivery.

Facing a bowler coming from around the wicket, his head is over off-stump.

Even the World's best batsmen get the occasional technical glitch.

Sir Alastair Cook (England and Essex CCC)

Late outswing here from West Indies paceman Kemar Roach getting Sir Alastair Cook to edge behind the wicket.

With Cook's bat behind his body and pointing towards fine-leg just after ball release, he has been forced to bring his bat down to access the ball in an arc around his body and against the late away-swing of the ball.

Left-hand batsman facing a right arm over bowler or left arm around wicket

- Head at ball release…

It helps to have the head over **middle/middle-and-leg stump** at ball release and it faces the bowler's hand. This helps for coping with the late in-swing, so often the major threat from this angle of delivery.

- Shoulder, hip and feet alignment …

The feet, hips and shoulders align towards the bowler's hand. The front leg and foot are slightly open for easier access to deliveries swinging back in towards the stumps.

- Hands and bat….

The hands and bat are kept close to the body (under the head) and close to the midriff to maintain good balance, control and for generating more power. The top hand and front elbow align to the bowler. The toe of the bat points upwards (unweighting) for a longer and more rhythmical swing and for easier control and to come down on top of shorter, bouncing deliveries. The bat is visible to the bowler throughout.

- Straight line from head, through hands to feet…

Creating an imaginary straight line from the head, through the hands to the feet at ball release, enables easy movement forward and back, to all lines of delivery and optimum control of the bat.

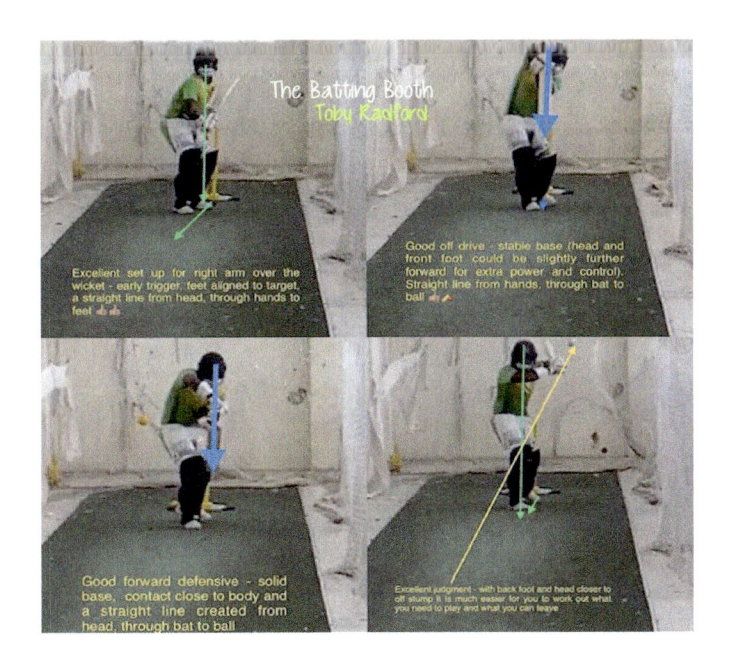

Leon Johnson (West Indies and Guyana)

West Indian batsman Leon Johnson has excellent alignment of hips, feet and shoulders when facing right-arm-over bowlers.

Rory Burns (England and Surrey CCC)

Aligning shoulders, hips, feet and the toe of the bat towards the bowler are important when left-handed batsmen face right arm bowlers from over the wicket.

This image shows Surrey opener Rory Burns aligning his front foot and bat towards mid-off when facing Middlesex seamer, Tim Murtagh, even though the ball was coming from the direction of mid-on.

This misalignment has forced Rory to bring his bat down in an arc from behind his head, and against the line of the ball, which left him with half a bat face at ball contact, and he edged to slip (image below)

Aligning his feet, shoulders and toe of the bat towards the bowler at ball release will help Rory.

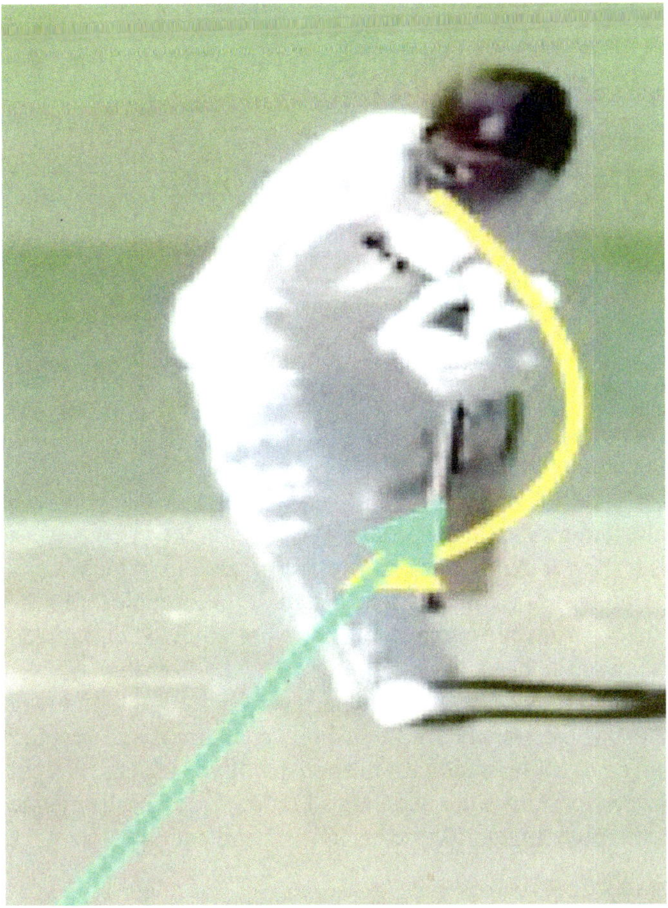

The Bat Tap / Pick up

Again, this is very personal. Some batsmen like to tap the bat, while others like to have it off the ground. Either is fine, as long as the top hand dominates the backswing and the bat path.

Hands and bat ideally will be close to the body (under the head) and at the midriff. A figure 9 is created between the shoulders, front elbow and the bat and this shape is maintained through all straight bat shots, in defence and attack.

In recent times, I have seen a lot of young players who start with the bat and hands close to their back hip, which limits the rhythm of a full swing, brings more weight closer to the back leg and tends to lead to a more bottom hand dominated swing of the bat.

Pointing the front elbow at the bowler's stumps and keeping the hands in the middle of the body subtly brings the weight further forward and encourages the top hand and front side of the body to control the backswing and bat path.

The Backswing

The backswing is part of the "step and swing" – the hands and bat being taken back as the body either moves forward or back to the ball.

Some players like to keep the bat low before they take it back (1-phase backswing), while others stand with the bat half way or even fully up before moving to the ball (2-phase backswing). It is personal choice and both can work very effectively.

Crucial is that the top hand dominates the final take back of the bat during the step forward or back to the ball. If the top hand controls the backswing it invariably controls the downswing and gives rhythm, control and timing to the shots.

The head and front shoulder dipping forward enable the hands and bat to go back and up – like the "cocking of a trigger" on a gun. Ready to explode on the shot.

For straight bat shots, the hands and bat will ideally be taken back close to the body, under the head and with the toe of the bat pointing upwards to "lighten" the bat and give extra rhythm to the bat path.

For pulls, sweeps and other cross bat shots, it is natural to take the hands back slightly further away from the body to create the room and leverage to swing the bat comfortably on a more horizontal plane.

Having the blade of the bat a fraction open helps create clean strike on both sides of the wicket. Too open a blade can lead to 'slicing the ball', while an excessively closed bat face can create contact with the ball on the inside edge. Ultimately, players need to find the blade position that gives them consistently clean contact with the ball on both sides of the wicket.

While some batsmen like to take the bat back in a straight line, others will loop the toe out and around towards third man before realigning it with the front shoulder and top hand to come down straight from the top of the backswing.

Batsmen who take the toe of the bat out towards third man in the backswing, look to keep the front elbow close to the body and at the top of the swing as the bat then realigns, they creates a straight line from the front shoulder, front elbow, top hand and, bat in the direction of the shot.

Hands are kept close to the body at ball release

Shimron Hetmeyer (West Indies and Guyana), Virat Kohli (India), Ed Joyce (Ireland, Sussex CCC)

The top hand controls the bat with the hands close to the body and under the head at ball release.

Why do the top players keep the bat close to the body?

- The bat becomes lighter (closer to the centre of mass) and keeps the body balanced
- It is easier to control and adjust the shot
- Can generate more power

Ideally, at ball release, there should be an imaginary straight line from the head, through the hands to the feet for optimum balance

The Backswing and Step

Dip front shoulder and head forward to take hands back and the toe of the bat upwards. - this "cocks the trigger" and gets the bat ready for the downswing

A great example here from Bangladesh team practice session of how to create the backswing.

As the head and front shoulder dip forward, the hands and bat are taken back. The toe of the bat points upwards to create a longer and more rhythmical swing.

A 'figure 9' is created between the shoulders, front arm and bat, which is maintained through all straight bat shots (backswing and bat path), in defence and attack.

A Rhythmical Backswing

England batsman Joe Root's effortless timing and control is largely due to his rhythmical backswing.

At ball release he points his front elbow forward and brings his hands close to his midriff. His top hand is level with his front thigh before it starts to smoothly swing the bat back.

As Joe moves his head and front shoulder forward to the ball, his hands and bat are then taken back and the toe of the bat points upwards (this gives a longer swing and helps to get on top of the bounce of the ball).

By having his top hand on the front thigh at ball release, Joe can create a fast and smooth swing of the bat backward and forward, much like a golfer swinging a club back from a mid-body starting position before striking the ball.

The long top-hand take-back gives great rhythm to Joe's swing and enables him to accelerate his hands and bat in attack and to decelerate them and play late with control in defence. (See image on page 74)

Joe Root

At ball release - front elbow points forward and top hand is level with front thigh

As his head and shoulder move forwards the hands are taken back and up (top hand to back hip) and the toe of the bat points upwards

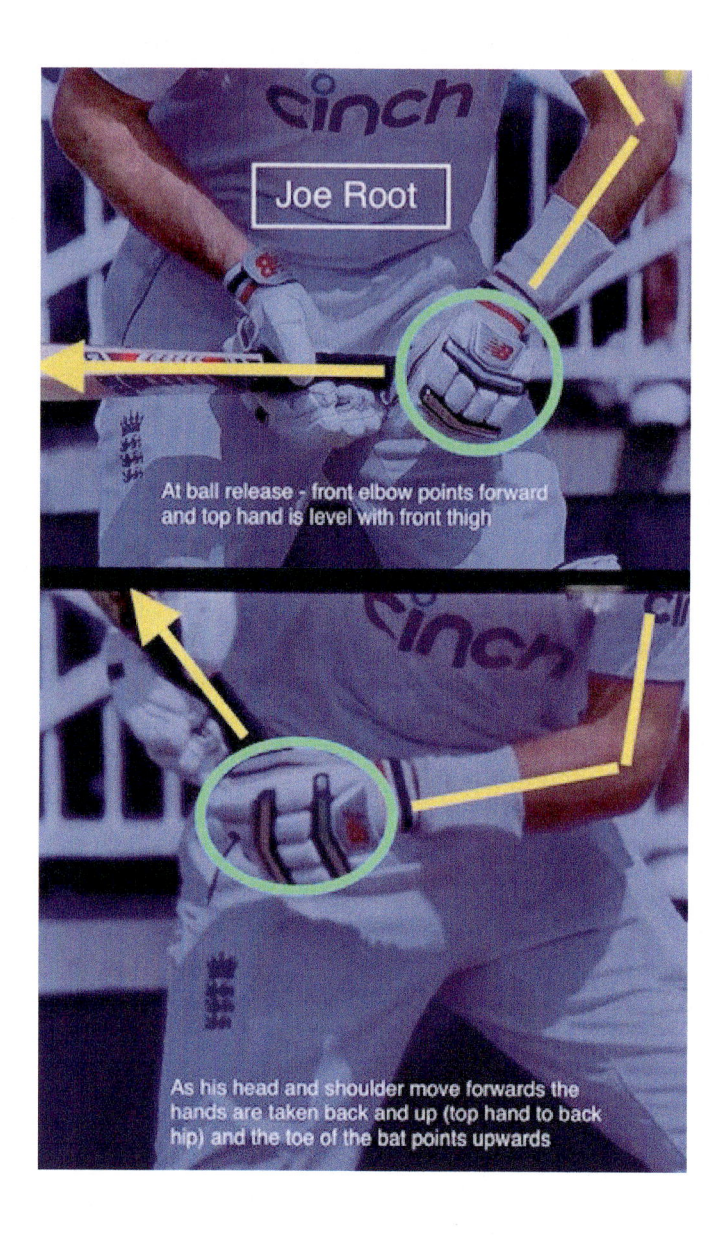

Subtle Changes

Kraigg Brathwaite (West Indies)

Subtle Changes – Players evolve their game as opposition teams try to expose perceived weaknesses.

Kraigg Brathwaite has worked hard to transform from the image on the left – hands away from his body and the toe of the bat hidden behind his back, which made accessing the ball with a straight bat path difficult and this caused a tendency to be dismissed lbw or caught behind the wicket. The image on the right shows Kraigg's back foot and head closer to off-stump, and his head facing the bowler's stumps, with his hands closer to his body, and the toe of his bat can be seen by the bowler.

With those subtle changes, Kraigg now has easier access to the ball on each side of the wicket and he is able to transfer his weight quicker, forward and back.

He is now tighter defensively and scoring on both sides of the ground.

Liam Dawson (England and Hampshire CCC)

Liam Dawson has brought his hands closer to his body and the toe of the bat from behind his back to point at first slip.

He is now able to access all lines of delivery and present a full face of the bat more consistently.

The Batting Booth — Toby Radford

Roston Chase

Roston Chase (West Indies)

Roston was placing a lot of weight on his back leg and taking his hands away from his body at ball release, which left him with a tendency to play with a "c shape" bat path, and being bowled or caught behind (Photo on left)

He is now more aligned, with his hips and shoulders towards the bowler's stumps and his hands close to his body and under his head at ball release (Photo on right)

Jacques Rudolph (South Africa and Glamorgan CCC)

Jacques got into a habit of taking his hands away from his body at ball release and this led to him playing with a "c shape" bat path.

When he kept his hands closer to his body he was tighter in defence and able to show his full range of elegant and exquisitely timed strokes.

Moving to the ball on the front foot ...

It is important at release of the ball, that the head and body weight remain forward and neutral (head towards bowler's stumps), giving the batsman the ability to move quickly to all lines of delivery.

The ball is tracked in flight and the head moves to the "finishing" line of the ball so that the appropriate base is created for the shot to be played.

As the hands move back in the backswing, as part of the "step and swing", while the head and front foot move forward towards the ball, it helps if the hands remain close to the body and under the line of the head. By keeping the hands under the head, it helps to create a straight bat path and to make easier adjustments of that bat path should the ball move late (swing, seam, spin).

Common problems...

- ❖ The head moves early towards the starting line of the ball and when the ball alters its line or length it becomes difficult to create a stable base in the appropriate position for the shot.

- ❖ The hands and bat are taken wide from the body during the backswing and step which can cause the head to move towards the off side and affect balance.

Drills ...

- For waiting longer at ball release ...

Trigger early and before release of the ball (throw, bowling machine, bowler) / maintain head position towards the bowler's stumps at ball release.

Use the bowling machine and face slow, large inswing deliveries. Meet the finishing line of the ball and hit them back at the bowler's stumps.

- Hands and bat under head during step and swing forward…

"Top hand only" bobble feed drills. Using the top hand only on the bat almost forces the hand to stay close to the body in the backswing because the bat becomes lighter and easier to control when it is closer to the centre of mass (the body).

Moving forward with his hands under his head

Darren Stevens (Kent CCC)
Darren Stevens pictured here during his fabulous innings of 190 from 149 deliveries for Kent against Glamorgan (2021).

His hands are kept close to his body and under his head as he moves onto the front foot.

Moving forward with hands under the head

A perfect example here of how the world's top batsmen keep their hands under their head as they move forward to play all their straight bat shots.

Ed Pollock (Worcestershire CCC)

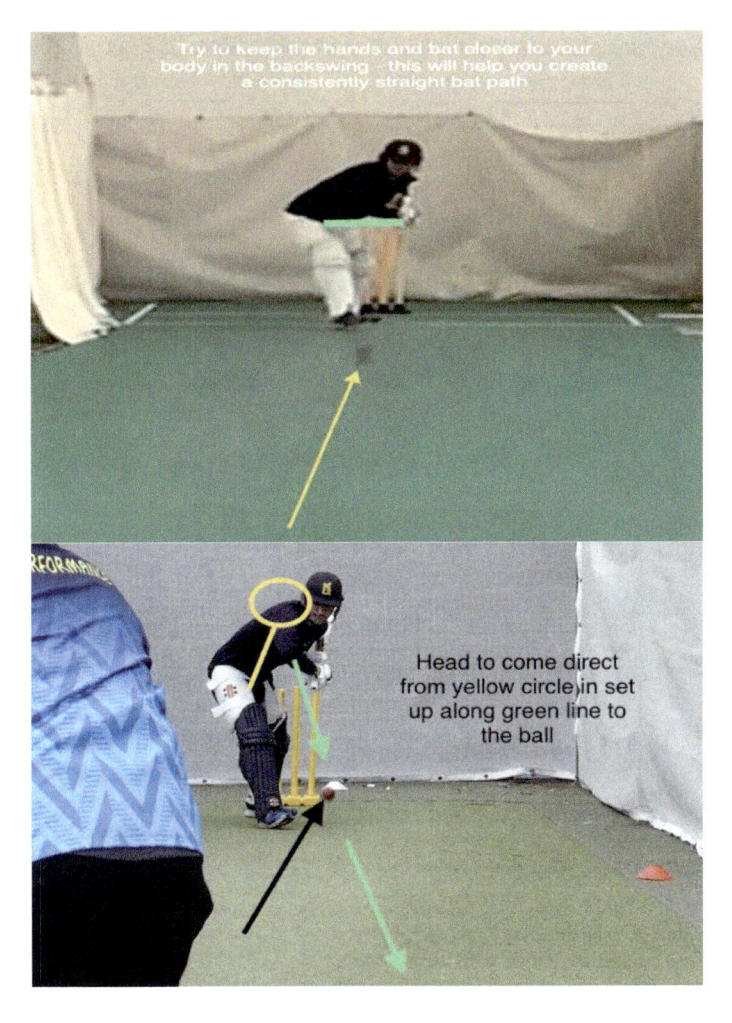

Try to keep the hands and bat closer to your body in the backswing - this will help you create a consistently straight bat path

Head to come direct from yellow circle in set up along green line to the ball

Worcestershire's dynamic batsman Ed Pollock continues to work hard on his head moving more directly to the line of the ball and keeping his hands closer to his body and under his head.

Prithvi Shaw (India)

Prithvi Shaw had a disappointing tour of Australia, with a run of low scores. He kept taking his hands a long way from his body (big top hand – front hip separation) which was affecting his balance and making him vulnerable to deliveries angling or moving back towards the stumps.

SHAW SURGES TOP
MOST RUNS IN A VIJAY HAZARE SEASON

movement. I was in a fixed position. I needed to keep my bat closer to my body, which I wasn't doing."

Prithvi Shaw (India)

It was wonderful to see Prithvi return to form a few months later after working hard to rectify the issue he had in Australia with his backswing.

He said: "I realised that I needed to keep my bat closer to my body, which I wasn't doing".

Prithvi went on to amass 754 runs in seven innings (average 188) for Mumbai.

It was great to see him working hard on his game and getting rewarded for it.

Playing from a stable base on the front foot

Making contact with the ball from a stable base helps to give control and maximise power in the shot.

Contact is made under or close to the head, with the head over or beyond the front foot. Bending the front knee and coming onto the inside of the back toe brings the head forward and ensures maximum bodyweight in the shot.

On straight bat attacking shots, the shoulders rotate vertically and the hands and bat accelerate through the line of the ball. On defensive straight bat shots, the hands and bat decelerate to allow the ball to hit the bat and drop close by.

Ideally, two straight lines are created at contact.

- (from side on) – line from head through front foot for control, timing and power.

- (from front on) – line from head through bat in direction of the shot for control of shot.

Common Problems…

- Contact is made with the head behind the front foot. Ball is often hit in the air or deliveries are edged to the wicket-keeper or slips.
- Shoulder rotation is slightly horizontal. This affects the length of time the bat face stays on the ball and leads to playing across the line (this can happen if the back toe, hips, or shoulder rotate too early in the bat path).
- Shot selection – player looking to drive deliveries that are not quite full enough. Need to be selective about

which deliveries can be driven and which have to be defended.

Drills ...

- "Hitting from a finishing position" is a very useful way to practice this shot as the batsman can position himself in the ideal place for connecting with the ball. Muscle memory is created with the head forward and over the front foot at contact, the front knee bent and the inside of the back toe in contact with the floor.

  The batsman positions himself with his head over his front foot for a straight drive.

  Hands and bat start at the top of the backswing. He hits drop feeds. Focus is on a vertical shoulder rotation and the acceleration of hands and bat through the line of the ball. This can be done for all front foot drives.

- "Rapid fire" drop feeds – encourage fast hands for generating speed and power through the ball.

- Top hand drills to encourage front shoulder / top hand control of the bat path. Focus is on contact from a stable base and with the head over the front foot.

Playing from a stable base on the front foot

A stable base enables control and power. Contact with the ball is made under the head, with the head over – or close to – the front foot.

From left to right Mushfiqur Rahim (Bangladesh), Ed Pollock (Worcestershire CCC), Ollie Pope (England and Surrey) and Najmul Shanto (Bangladesh)

Chris Gayle (West Indies)

Chris Gayle demonstrates here that when playing forward, coming onto the inside toe of the back foot (lifting the heel off the ground), helps his head and bodyweight to go further forward into the shot.

Contact with the ball can then take place under his head for optimum control, power and timing.

Really solid - love that you've got your head and front foot into the ball and a lovely straight line from head through hands to ball. Top shot

Shane DOWRICH
Emirates Old Trafford // 22 July

Shane Dowrich (West Indies)

A good forward defensive shot – Shane is stable at ball contact and has created a straight line from his head, through the hands and bat to the ball

Ollie Pope (England and Surrey CCC)

Ollie Pope playing here from a stable base. Contact is made under his head which is over his front foot. He has maintained the "figure 9" through the shot.

Australian club cricketers and clients of the Batting Booth

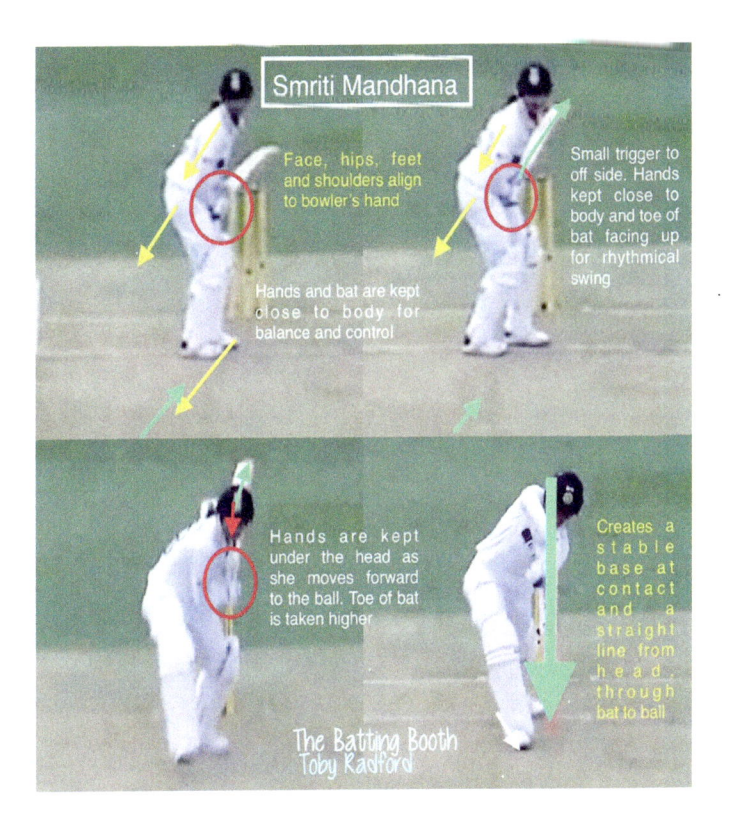

Smriti Mandhana (India)

A beautiful straight drive here from India star Smriti Mandhana during a brilliant century (127) against Australia women.

Smriti is wonderfully balanced at the crease and aligns her face, feet, hips and shoulders to the bowler's hand at ball release.

- She keeps her hands close to her body and under her head for optimum balance and control

- As she moves her head and front foot forward to the ball, her hands remain under her head as the toe of the bat is taken higher to create a rhythmical swing

- She connects with the ball from a stable base and under her head and creates an imaginary straight line from her head, through the bat to the ball

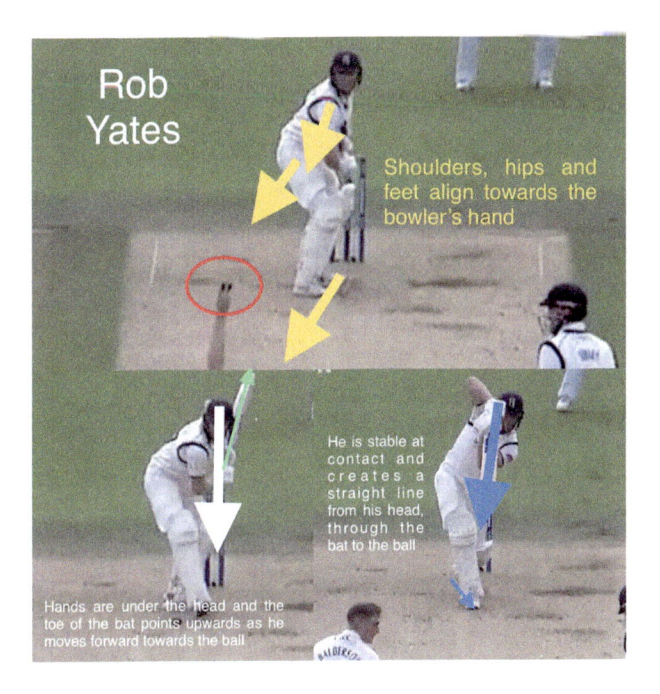

Rob Yates (Warwickshire CCC)

A terrific straight drive from Warwickshire's Rob Yates during his hundred (113) against Lancashire.

Rob – facing a right-arm-over bowler – aligns his face, hips and feet towards the bowler's hand at ball release.

As he moves forward to the ball, he keeps his hands close to his body and under his head (for optimum balance and control) and the toe of the bat points upwards for a rhythmical swing.

Rob is stable as he accelerates his hands and bat through the line of the ball and makes contact under his head.

He creates an imaginary straight line from his head, through his hands to the ball.

Keagan Simmons (Trinidad)

Keagan will benefit from getting his front hip and front foot closer to the line of the ball to create a more solid base at contact. This will help him present a full bat face at the ball and prevent the bat from turning at contact.

The back foot remains flat at ball contact here (green circle), which prevents all the body weight and power getting into the stroke.

Keeping the back leg straight and coming onto the inside of the left toe (heel off the floor) will bring more body weight into the shot and the head over the front foot at contact for greater control, timing and power.

From a Straight Line to a Straight line

Top batsmen move from a balanced position in their set-up to a balanced position at ball contact.

They look to create a straight line in the set-up (from their head, through their hands to their feet) and a straight line in their straight bat shots in both defence and attack (from their head, through the hands and bat, to the ball)

Babar Azam (Pakistan)

Pakistan's brilliant Babar Azam gives a wonderful example here of the straight line at ball release to a straight line at ball contact.

Marnus Labuschagne (Australia)

Marnus Labuschagne - from a straight line at ball release to a straight line at ball contact

Devon Conway (NZ) - From a Straight Line at ball release to a Straight Line at Ball contact

Jason Holder (West Indies)

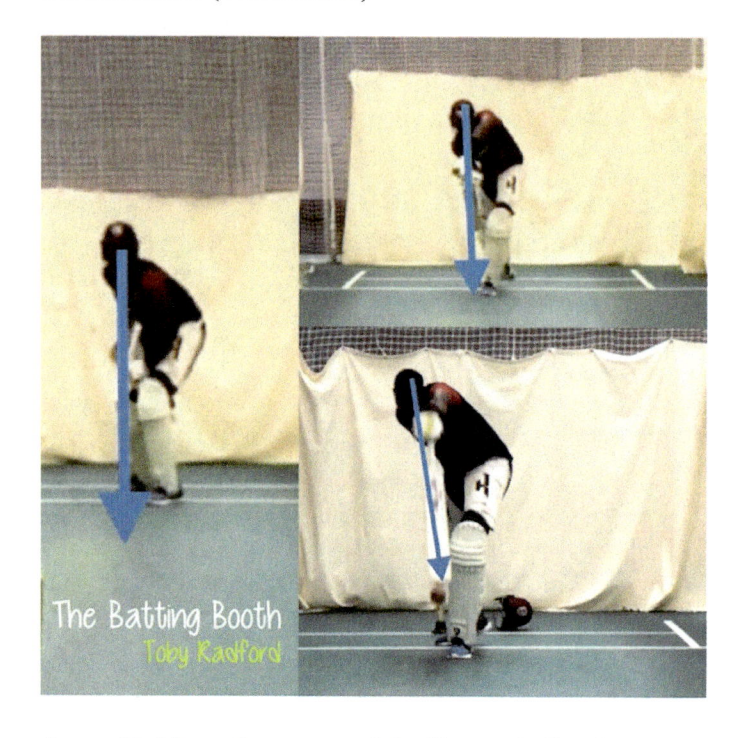

Jason Holder - from a straight line at ball release to a straight line at ball contact

Moving to the ball on the back foot ...

It is important at release of the ball, that the head and bodyweight remain forward and neutral (head towards bowler's stumps) – giving the batsman the ability to move quickly to all lengths and lines of delivery.

Once the length has been judged as short, the hands and bat are taken back in the backswing – as part of the "step and swing" and the back foot moves quickly backwards to the off side.

The hands remain close to the body and under the line of the head. By keeping the hands under the head, it helps to create a straight bat path and to make easier adjustments of that bat path should the ball move late (swing, seam, spin).

Common problems…

- ❖ The head moves first to the ball rather than the back foot and there is a lack of balance at contact.

- ❖ The hands and bat are taken wide from the body during the backswing and step which can also affect balance at contact.

Drills …

Hands and bat under head during step and swing back …

- "The back foot catch drill" – lob a catch, which must be taken by the bottom hand, under the head and from the appropriate stable base on the back foot.

- Top hand only full toss and bounce-fed drills. Using the top hand only on the bat, almost forces the hand and bat to stay close to the body in the backswing because the bat becomes lighter and easier to control when it is closer to the centre of mass (the body).

Playing from a stable base on the back foot

Making contact with the ball from a stable base helps to give control and maximise power in the shot.

Contact is made close to the head. The head and front shoulder dip forward to maintain good balance.

On straight bat attacking shots, the shoulders rotate vertically and the hands and bat accelerate through the line of the ball. On defensive straight bat shots, the hands and bat decelerate to allow the ball to hit the bat and drop close by.

Ideally, a straight line is created at contact - from the head through the bat in the direction of the shot (for control of shot)

Common Problems…

- ❖ Contact is made with the head outside the line of the back foot. Ball is often hit in the air or bat path is forced across the line of the ball.

- ❖ Shoulder rotation slightly horizontal. This affects the length of time the bat face stays on the ball and leads to playing across the line (can happen if back toe, hip or shoulder rotates too early in the bat path).

Drills …

- "Hitting from a finishing position" is a very useful way to work on the back foot straight bat shots. The player places himself in the ideal position for connecting with the ball. Muscle memory is created with the head and front shoulder dipped forward, a stable side-on base (back foot parallel to the crease), the hands and bat back with the toe of the bat facing upwards.

With the hands and bat starting at the top of the backswing, full toss underarm feeds are forced in the direction of extra cover. Focus is placed on a vertical shoulder rotation and the acceleration of hands and bat through the line of the ball. A deceleration of hands and bat are required for the backfoot defensive.

- Top hand drills moving from a normal stance position to encourage the step and swing and front shoulder / top hand control of the backswing and bat path. Focus is on vertical shoulder rotation, contact being made from a stable base close to the head, and the head and front shoulder remaining dipped forward.

Look to defend stump deliveries with the head and back foot behind the line of the ball and not at the side of the ball

Joe Root (England and Yorkshire CCC)

Whenever playing deliveries targeting the stumps – on front or back foot – in attack or defence – look to play with the head and back foot behind the line of the ball, as seen here with England's Joe Root (picture far right).

Playing straight deliveries with the back foot (red circle) and head behind the line of the ball helps to create a straight bat path and gives a second line of defence.

Ideally, a straight line should be created from the head, through the bat to the ball (yellow arrow).

Playing straight deliveries at the side of the body and the head, makes edging behind the wicket a real possibility (pictures 1 and 2).

Contact is made at the side of the body when playing deliveries outside off-stump and those moving down the leg side.

The Square Cut

Played to a short delivery wide of off-stump. The back foot moves back and across to the off side as the hands and bat are taken back. The toe of the bat points upwards so that it can come down on top of the bounce of the ball.

A rotation of the front shoulder prepares the bat to start its horizontal swing. The hands and bat accelerate through the line of the ball and contact is made as the ball passes through an imaginary box that runs parallel with the back foot. The ball is hit square on the off side.

Common Problems.

- ❖ Head and bodyweight slightly back on the shot
- ❖ Bat path from low to high which hits the ball in the air
- ❖ Contact is made early with the bottom hand dominating the bat path and a closed bat face presented to the ball.
- ❖ Trying to cut deliveries that are too tight or angling back into the stumps – these need to be played with a straight bat rather than a cross bat

Drills…

- From a finishing position (back foot back and across, rotated front shoulder and hands and bat taken back and up), hit full toss feeds square on the off side.
- Progress to hitting from a stance position
- Progress to hitting bounced feeds. Feed from both sides of the wicket

The Square Cut

Feroze Khushi (Essex CCC)

A wonderful square cut from Feroze Khushi. His back foot has moved back and across to get his head close to the line of the ball. From a stable base, he has rotated his shoulders and accelerated his hands and bat through the line of the ball.

The Pull Shot / Pivot-Pull

Playing the short-pitched delivery from a medium pace bowler or spinner offers time and the opportunity to position the feet deep in the crease to play the 'text book' pull shot.

When facing fast bowling where reaction time is reduced, the pivot pull, with subtle weight transfer, minimal foot movement and fast hands, can generate exceptional power and speed.

A 'punch' of the hands at ball contact adds to the pace on the ball and makes it a highly effective shot against the short ball bowled at high speed.

The head and front shoulder dip forward to take the hands and the toe of the bat high. The head remains forward at ball contact to maintain good balance in the shot. The front foot can come off the floor to create a counter-balance at contact.

The shoulders rotate horizontally and the bat and hands accelerate through the ball – contact is made at full arm's length with the bat moving from high to low to keep the ball down.

Common Problems..

- ❖ Head and bodyweight are sightly back at contact so no stable base created.

- ❖ Bat path is from low to high and the ball travels in the air

- ❖ Trying to hit against the angle of the ball – it is easier sometimes for a right hand batsman to hit a left arm bowler through the off side than to try to drag the ball back against the angle and into the leg side.

Drills ..

- For a consistent strike from high to low and at arm's length, hit underarm full-toss deliveries from a front-on position with the hands and bat starting at top of backswing.

- Head remains still at contact and the ball is hit hard just in front of square on the leg side

- Progress to normal stance and move into position for the pull / pivot pull

- Throw / fling / feed bowling machine / bowl – to practise the pull. Mix lengths to make decision-making, foot movement and weight transfer as realistic and as sharp as possible. Feed from both sides of the wicket.

David Lloyd (Glamorgan CCC)

Top Glamorgan batsman David Lloyd gives an excellent example of how to play the pivot-pull as he hits an enormous six against Middlesex in their T20 clash.

- Head and bodyweight are forward at ball release and early ball flight for quick transfer of weight

- Hands and bat are kept close to the body, with the toe of the bat pointing up and visible to the bowler for easy access to the ball

- Head remains still as the shoulders rotate and the hands and bat accelerate through the shot for power.

Devon Conway (New Zealand)

A wonderful pivot-pull here from New Zealand's Devon Conway during his brilliant century against Bangladesh.

- Devon's hands and bat stay close to his body and under his head for balance and control until he has judged the line and length of the ball

- He takes his hands and bat away from his body to create the horizontal bat path and leverage for the cross-batted stroke. The toe of the bat points upwards in the backswing to enable the bat to hit down on the ball (control)

- Devon's shoulders rotate horizontally and he makes contact with the ball at full arm's length. The hands and bat accelerate through the ball as the bat comes from high to low to keep the ball down. His head remains forward and still throughout.

Playing against deliveries that angle back into the stumps – swing / seam

When playing any full delivery that angles or moves back in towards the stumps – spin / seam or swing – it is important not to commit the head and front foot to the early line of the ball but, instead, to wait and meet the line it finishes on.

Having the head to meet the end line of the ball, enables contact to take place from the appropriate stable position and under the head for optimum control and timing.

For right-handed batsmen facing right arm over bowlers, the face and body will ideally align to the bowler's stumps. The eyes will track the angle of the delivery from the hand but there will be no early commitment of head, front foot or body weight towards it or to the off-side.

Most problems playing deliveries that are angled in, come from an early commitment to the starting line of the ball. Once the head moves in that direction, the front foot then aligns towards mid-off as it lands across the wicket.

As the ball then moves back into the stumps, the head – having committed early to the initial line – ends up outside the line the ball finishes on, and the only way for the bat to connect with it is to come across the line (with less blade) from the off-side.

International bowlers vary where they deliver from on the crease as they try to set up a batsman. They will often bowl a number of deliveries from close to the stumps and into the off-stump channel. Looking to encourage an early commitment of the batsman's head and front foot towards the off-side, the bowler will then deliver from wide of the crease and angle it back in towards the stumps. Chris Woakes and Stuart Broad are both excellent exponents of 'setting up' batsmen in this fashion.

Common Problems

- ❖ Head moves early to starting line of the ball and finishes outside the finishing line of the ball. Bat path is forced to come across the line of the ball, leading to dismissal by lbw/ bowled / caught mid-wicket etc.

Drills

- To help batsman to wait and to meet the finishing line of the ball - set up the bowling machine to deliver big in-swinging full deliveries. With top hand only, look to drive the ball back from a stable base with the head over the front foot through two cones positioned either side of the bowler's stumps.

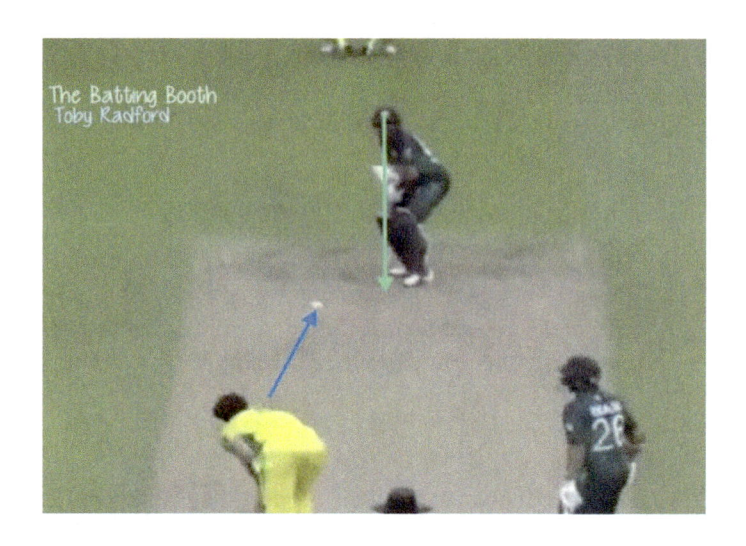

Babar Azam (Pakistan)

Babar Azam is beautifully balanced here and waiting to spring into action well after the ball has left the bowler's hand.

Babar keeps his hands close to his body, his head forward (close to off-stump) and his body aligned to the bowler's stumps.

By tracking the path of the ball, but not committing early towards it with his head or feet in this way, Babar can then move quickly and easily to the appropriate balanced position when the ball finally reaches him.

This is wonderful skill and technique and one of the main reasons why Babar Azam is ranked ICC number one batsman in the world in both ODI and T20 format and is world number seven in Test cricket.

Ollie Pope (England and Surrey CCC)

Ollie Pope was lbw in England's first innings against New Zealand at Lord's in June 2021 because his head moved early to the starting line of the ball, which forced him to play across the line.

To play deliveries that are angling, swinging or seaming back in, the head needs to be inside the line of off-stump (blue circle), and meet the finishing line of the ball in order to present a full bat face.

Playing against deliveries that move away from the bat – swing or seam

Playing any moving ball - swing, seam or spin – requires the head to move towards the finishing line of the ball. Waiting at ball release and tracking the ball in its early flight, is key.

Wait and play late. Let the ball move and allow it to come close to you. Connect under the head and from a stable base.

Late away swing – the type that has brought England's Jimmy Anderson a record-breaking number of Test Match wickets - is difficult to play, especially when deliveries move from the stump line or angle in towards the stumps before then swinging away sharply in the opposite direction.

Maintaining a relatively sideways on body position enables the front shoulder and top hand to bring the bat down in a straight line.

Looking to play as straight as possible on the leg side and avoiding the temptation to play square of the wicket against the swing helps to present a full bat face to the ball.

Many top international batsmen position their head close to off-stump at ball release to help them judge the deliveries they can leave and those they need to play.

Any ball therefore that pitches and moves from outside the line of their head (off-stump or wider) can be left comfortably. For those pitching slightly straighter, allowing the ball to swing and then connecting with it under the head and close to the body gives control to the shot. If the bat finds the edge of a ball that has been played late in this fashion, it often goes into the ground and square of the wicket. Rarely will it carry for a catch.

Players who stand further to the leg side at ball release and move across the wicket to get close to off-stump and channel deliveries often find it more difficult to judge which ones to play at and which ones they can leave. When they do play, it tends to be more across the wicket and with less width of bat presented to the ball. This makes them more vulnerable to edging behind the wicket to the wicket-keeper or slips.

For those batsmen who position with their head closer to off-stump, it helps them to defend with a fuller bat face, if they can move their head and body directly to the finishing line of the ball – moving down the wicket - rather than across it.

A very simple but useful drill for practising defending in and around off-stump is to position a cone on the line of straight extra cover about two yards down from the crease line and a yard outside the line of off-stump.

If the batsmen feels that a delivery can only be defended square of, and outside the cone, then it is a ball that should be left. Any defensive shots should be played inside the line of the cone. Quite quickly, players work out what to play and what to leave, and when they do defend they do so by moving more directly to the ball rather than across the wicket where the outside edge of the bat becomes more exposed.

When driving against away swing, it is important to make sure the ball is close to the head at contact. Turning the front shoulder in the direction of the swing keeps the front side of the body in control of the shot and helps to present a fuller bat face with the movement of the ball.

Striking a short-pitched or back of a length delivery that shapes away after pitching also requires the front shoulder to turn to hit with the movement. As the ball gets wider, the straight bat forcing shot off the back foot through extra cover then becomes a cut square of the wicket on the off side – again with the front shoulder turning in the direction of the swing to align the bat for the stroke.

When playing on the back foot to off-stump and channel deliveries, batsmen need to be instinctive with their judgment of when to leave, when to play with a straight bat through mid-off and extra cover and when the cross bat square cut presents more bat to the ball and is the safer option.

Using the bowling machine to deliver a number of balls on this length and line and subtly altering the amount of away swing, helps the batsman to become confident with his judgment and shot selection.

Common problems…

- ❖ The head is too far back or too far outside the line of the feet at contact, preventing a stable base and optimum balance in the shot

- ❖ The body is too open at contact, back toe, hip and shoulder rotating to face down the wicket, leading to a bat path dominated by the bottom hand. This makes it difficult to bring the bat down in a straight line.

Drills…

- Cone drill (as above)

- Bowling machine – altering starting line of the ball and the amount of swing. Judgment of what to play and appropriate contact point improves through practice. Front shoulder to turn into the direction of the shot to enable a straight bat path

Connor Brown (Glamorgan CCC and Wales Minor County)

A simple "off-stump channel" drill with Glamorgan's Connor Brown.

If the ball cannot be defended comfortably inside the blue cone with a full, straight blade, then it is a ball to leave.

Judgment in and around off-stump soon becomes much more consistent and the defence tighter.

A simple, but very effective drill.

Playing Swing – Playing Late

Playing Swing – Playing Late

The image above shows potential ball tracking from a right arm over delivery (yellow curved line) and a left arm over delivery (green curved line)

As the ball meets the batsman in the same place (red circle), the same shot is played to both deliveries – on the front foot from a stable base back straight.

An imaginary straight line is created from the head, through the bat to the ball (blue arrow) and a full face of the bat is presented to the ball.

Playing Swing – Playing Late

From Right Arm Over – Yellow Curve –

Track the ball from the bowler's hand and in its early stages of flight (the first two yellow balls in image) and move the head and front foot to the finishing line of the ball at contact (red circle)

From Left Arm Over – Green Curve –

Track the ball from the bowler's hand and in its early stages of flight (the first two red balls in image) and move the head and front foot to the finishing line of the ball at contact (red circle)

Playing spin...
Advancing down the wicket....

Fast and nimble footwork are attributes held by all good players of spin bowling. The best players also judge the flight and the length of the ball well and then use their nimble footwork to get close to the ball on the front foot or to push back quickly to give them extra time and space to play the shot.

Most players will take a guard slightly more towards off-stump when facing the ball turning into the stumps (to help them play with the direction of spin), and stand slightly more towards leg stump for spinners turning the ball away from the bat to give them room to play through the off side.

Batsmen advance down the wicket to get close to the pitch of the ball and negate any spin. The first step is usually straight and large and the head and front shoulder dip forward to allow the hands and bat to be taken back and high in the step and swing (the toe of the bat upwards).

As with the front foot shots against pace bowling, the head moves to the finishing line of the ball on the front foot against spin. This allows the front foot to position itself just inside the ball and for the bat to have a clean and clear pathway to the ball.

Most current day batsmen click their feet together as they advance down the wicket to maintain the alignment of their body – hips, feet and shoulders - towards the target area. Creating a stable base close to the ball allows the head to be still as the arms and bat swing in a straight line. Contact for drives and defensive shots is made under the head for control, timing and power.

Common problems …

- The head is outside the line of the ball at contact, which forces the bottom hand to dominate the bat path and the bat to come across the line of the ball.

- The head is behind the front foot at contact. Contact with the ball is made early and too far in front of the body with the bottom hand dominating the bat path. This results in the ball being hit in the air.

Drills…

- Top hand only front foot drives against dropped and then lobbed feeds – this reinforces the head and front shoulder moving to the finishing line of the ball. Contact to be made with the head over the front foot from a stable base.

- To hit with the spin through the off side, the shoulders, feet and hips turn to align in the direction of the shot (past or over extra cover / mid-off

Playing spin

Jacob Blades (Glamorgan Academy and Wales U13)

Jacob Blades gives a good example here of how to advance down the wicket. He clicks his feet to maintain alignment of feet, hips and shoulders in the direction of the shot.

Jacob is balanced at ball contact, with his head over his front foot for control and timing.

Hitting Over The Top

Babar Azam (Pakistan)   Hitting Over The Top ...

A wonderful example here from Babar Azam against Australia using his feet to hit the off-spinner from a good length outside off-stump, with the spin over long on.

Babar takes his back foot well outside off-stump to enable his head to get close to the line of the ball. He aligns his feet in the direction of the shot (long on).

He dips his front shoulder to raise the toe of the bat and to create the backswing.

The shoulders rotate vertically as the hands and bat accelerate through the ball.

He keeps his head still and close to the ball and his body-weight forward for optimum control and timing

The blade is upright at contact to create elevation.

Kieran Powell (West Indies and Leeward Islands)

West Indies opening batsman Kieran Powell is beautifully balanced at ball contact after using his feet quickly to get to the pitch of the ball.

He creates a stable base, with his head over his front foot, and presents a full face of the bat at the ball.

Saif Hassan (Bangladesh)

Bangladesh top order batsman Saif Hassan creating an angle here to hit past and over mid-off – a turn of the front shoulder and the back elbow tucking inside enable him to "open" the bat face at contact. Great skill.

Playing against Spin ... Sweep shots

The Orthodox Sweep...

The sweep is often played to a good length ball, on or just outside the line of the stumps. The head and front foot position themselves on the line of the ball and contact is made with the head over the front foot and with the shoulders, arms and bat swinging horizontally from a high to low position to keep the ball down.

Contact is made at full arm's length and the ball is hit anywhere between backward square leg to deep mid-wicket. If the ball lands fuller than the ideal good sweeping length, then it is important to control the speed of the bat and angle of bat face to make contact.

During a sweeping session I will ask the batsmen which length (where on the pitch) they feel they are most comfortable controlling the sweep from (they mark a chalk area on the practice pitch to highlight "their" ideal sweeping zone)

Drills...

Progressive drill for the sweep shot...

1 – Batsman hits lobbed feeds from his sweep "finishing position" (back leg on ground, head over the front foot and bat at top of backswing with toe of bat facing up)

2 – As contact becomes consistently clean, the batsman then moves back into his normal stance and moves into the "finishing position" as deliveries are lobbed onto the sweep length.

3 – Feeds are gradually taken back until they become normal 'over arm' and delivered from a full pitch length.

A well controlled sweep. Head is forward and still at contact. Hands and bat have come from high to low to hit down on the ball

Kieran Powell (West Indies and Leeward Islands)

The Slog Sweep ...

With the slog sweep, the head moves to the finishing line of the ball and the front leg moves inside the line of the ball to create plenty of room for the bat to swing cleanly.

From a high backswing, with the toe of the bat pointing upwards, the bat path is a 'chopping motion' at approximately 45 degrees.

The head and body weight drive forward in the direction of the shot and contact is made just in front of the body. The head and weight need to stay forward.

The front leg often braces and the back leg bends slightly as power is generated through the shot. If the head or the weight is taken too much onto the back leg prior to, or at, contact, there is a loss of control and power in the shot.

Many players try to hit the slog sweep too hard and, in doing so, take their head and bodyweight backwards at contact. Contact with the ball is made early and there is a loss of control and power in the shot.

Like the orthodox sweep, players start to work out where they are comfortable for the ball to pitch for them to be able to strike the slog sweep cleanly and with full control.

The slog sweep is often the go-to boundary option when quick runs are needed. It can become a premeditated shot, for clearing the mid-wicket boundary or splitting the gap between mid-wicket and long-on / mid-wicket and square leg.

When players know exactly where their ideal "slog sweep box" is on the pitch, when they need quick runs and an element of shot pre-meditation is required, the box provides the perfect yardstick / guideline for the stroke.

If the ball lands in 'their area', they can commit fully to it and strike it cleanly high and hard over deep mid-wicket. If it is not in the right area, they take the sensible and simple option and then wait until a delivery pitches in the box for them to commit fully to it.

I believe that the best players premeditate their hitting this way. They are looking for a certain shot but only play it if the ball lands in their ideal part of the pitch. They have a plan B if the delivery doesn't. Conversely, slightly lesser players premeditate a big stroke and often regardless of where it lands commit to that initial stroke. They have no plan B or "get out of jail' shot and are often dismissed because of it.

Drills….

Progressive drill.

1 – A lobbed feed from the off-side into the ideal slog sweep area.

2 – Feeds progress to overarm and from a greater distance as consistency of strike improves.

Other useful spin drills…

1 – A useful drill – especially for one-day cricket – helps players to score low-risk singles against spin by hitting the three parts of the ground where fielders are usually positioned on the boundary (especially in shorter format cricket). These are a back foot punch to deep cover (slightly short delivery), a sweep or clip to deep square leg (full or

short straighter delivery) and using quick footwork to drive a flighted delivery to long-on or long-off.

Initially the coach can call the shot he wants played. As execution becomes consistent, the batsman then makes his / her own decision as to which of the three simple single options they take.

2 – For a slightly more advanced version, boundary options can be included and, also different coloured balls, which are to be hit in certain areas or on just one side of the pitch.

Both of the drills above encourage quick thinking, quick feet and help to create a clear game plan for scoring freely against spin bowling.

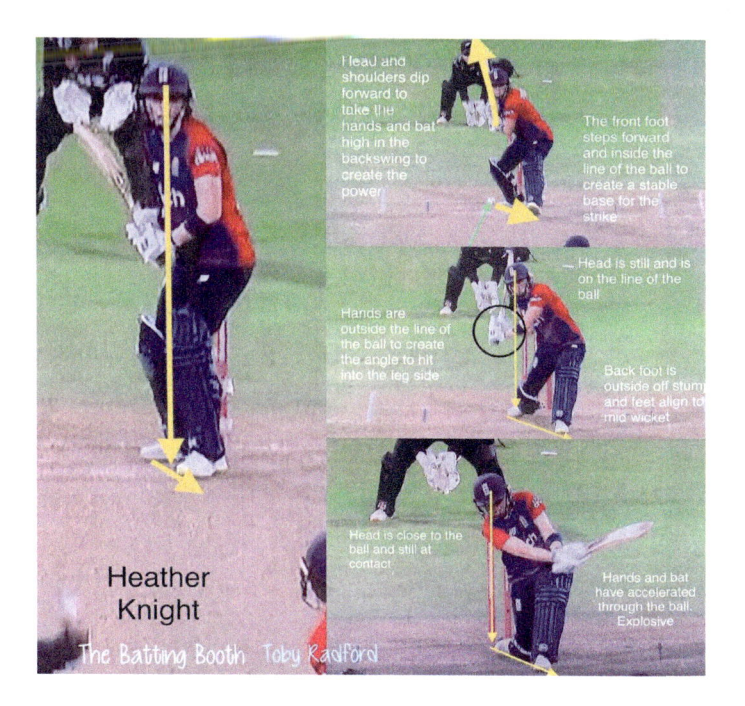

Heather Knight (England)

Just before ball release, Heather takes her back foot back and across outside off-stump. She gets her head outside off-stump and aligns her feet in the direction of the shot to the leg side.

Heather dips her head and shoulders forward to create a high backswing (her hands outside the line of the ball) as her front foot steps forward inside the line of the ball.

Heather creates a stable base and keeps her head still as she accelerates her hands and bat through the ball, up and over mid-wicket. Explosive.

The Slog Sweep

Kieran Powell (West Indies and Leeward Islands)

Power Hitting

The biggest and best hitters in the modern game all have the three B's – Base, Balance and Bat speed.

Striking with a still head position and from a balanced and stable base, helps with clean contact and timing and the transfer of energy and power through the shot.

Fast hands enable the bat to accelerate through the ball quickly to add further power to the stroke.

Many top batsmen - when looking for big boundaries – adopt a position in the crease at ball release which helps them to hit 360 degrees around the ground.

Former T20 World Cup winning West Indies batsman Marlon Samuels was one of the first I saw to adopt this now common striking position of taking the back foot back outside off-stump at ball release and opening the body and front foot into a very "front on" position.

This set-up having the back foot outside off-stump helps for reaching any wider deliveries. These can be sliced over or through the off side. With the open front foot, any straight deliveries can be accessed easily to be hit back down the ground or struck into (or over) the leg side, when angled in.

Marlon had great success with this powerful hitting position at the back end of T20 and One-day innings. He struck 52 runs from the last 19 balls he faced in the world T20 final against Sri Lanka.

Many have adopted Marlon's hitting stance. It is commonplace today in the shorter formats of the game.

Drills

1 – The batsman moves into his 'open' set-up, with his back foot at off-stump and his front foot outside leg as the bowler bounds to the wicket. The ball is fed in a variety of lengths and lines – either thrown or from a bowling machine – and the objective is for the batsman to react quickly, make good decisions as to which attacking option to take and to execute it well.

2 – Slower deliveries, slower bouncers and yorkers are to be added to make the drill as realistic as possible.

Andre Russell (West Indies)

Andre Russell is one of the biggest and cleanest strikers in the game, and he is seen here hitting a towering six in Australia's Big Bash.

- After ball release, his hands and bat are under his head and close to his body for control and to generate power, and his shoulders and hips align towards the bowler's stumps

- Andre's head and shoulders dip forwards as his hands and bat are taken back and up in the backswing. His hands remain under his head and his front foot opens in the direction of the shot – towards mid-wicket.

- Andre's front foot lands and creates a stable base to generate the power. His hips and shoulders rotate quickly against a braced front leg and his hands and bat accelerate through the line of the ball. Andre's head remains very still to enable a clean ball contact

Hitting Technique

Jason Holder **A B de Villiers** **Marlon Samuels**
(West Indies) **(SA)** **(West Indies)**

Batting at the Death

The modern batsman often positions his back foot across to the off-stump while opening his front foot, to enable easy access to all lines of delivery and scoring options on both sides of the wicket.

Jason Holder, A B de Villiers and Marlon Samuels show here how they can score all around the wicket (360 degrees) from this well-balanced set-up.

The "Helicopter Shot"

Rashid Khan (Afghanistan)

Rashid Khan's exciting "helicopter shot" employs good basic hitting technique.

1. Back foot and head are taken outside off-stump and the front foot is left "open"

2. Arms and bat accelerate through the ball as he creates a "snap" against a braced font leg for power.

3. Head remains still at contact

4. Head remains still after contact

Saif Hassan and Parvez Emon (Bangladesh)

I love the position that top young Bangladesh batsmen – Saif Hassan and Parvez Emon – take up at ball release when looking to hit boundaries.

- **Head and back foot on off-stump** – helps to reach wider deliveries and creates the angle to hit straight and on the leg side (score all around the ground)

- **Feet open and facing mid-on / mid-wicket** – creates easy access to straighter deliveries and is a powerful hitting position.

The Batting Booth

Some of the Success Stories so far ...

Nkrumah Bonner SOS!

West Indies top-order batsman, Nkrumah Bonner, rang me from Antigua early one morning, deeply concerned about his technique, especially as they had to bat all day to save the first Test against Sri Lanka.

I asked him to send me some recent video footage of him batting, and I would give him some advice to work on anything that might be needed in the nets before start of play.

It was immediately clear that Bonner was playing across the ball. Suranga Lakmal, in particular, was bowling wide of the crease, yet Bonner's left shoulder was almost facing mid-off.

The talented Jamaican needed to 'open' his left shoulder and hit straight at the stumps.

He also needed to move his guard slightly to middle-and-leg.

To help, I sent him an excellent photograph of South African batsman, AB de Villiers in the perfect set-up for him to study.

He worked on this advice in the nets immediately he received it, and then went out and scored his maiden Test century (113 not out), and West Indies drew the match.

Opening his shoulder allowed Nkrumah to bring the bat down straight.

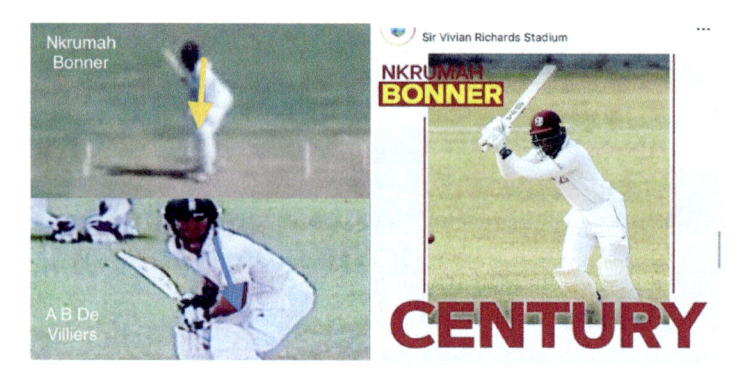

Rovman Powell (West Indies)

Great to see my old mate Rovman Powell play such an extraordinary innings for the West Indies in their T20 International. Such a talent and a great guy, too.

Jermaine Blackwood (West Indies)

Well done to Jermaine Blackwood on his hundred for the West Indies against New Zealand. He's a triumph for hard work, positivity and natural talent.

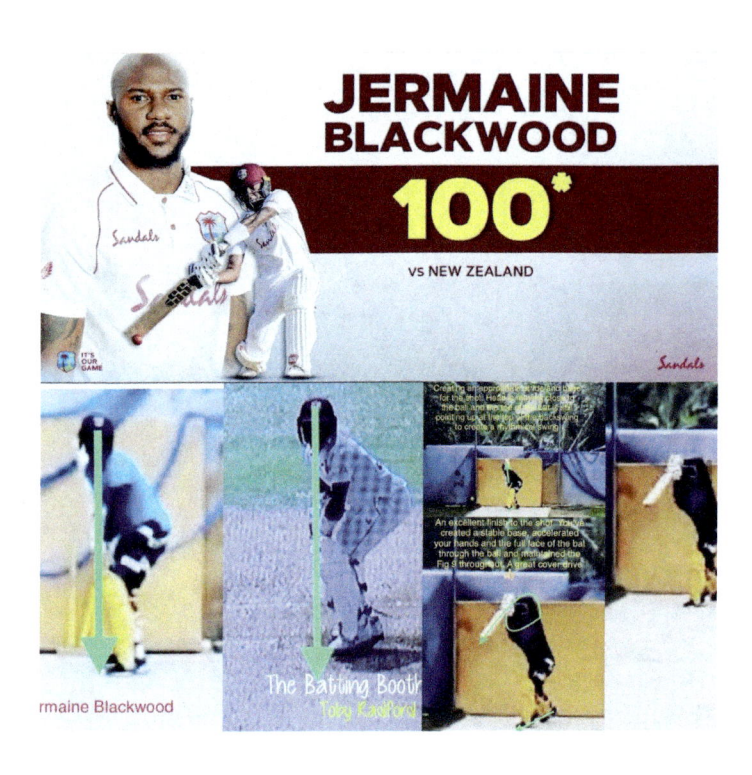

Najmul Shanto (Bangladesh)

I was delighted when Bangladesh High Performance batsman Najmul Shanto scored a century for the senior international team against Zimbabwe in Harare.

Feroze Khushi (Essex CCC)

Feroze Khushi worked very hard on his set-up and position at ball release. It was great when he made his debut century for Essex CCC in the Royal London One-Day Cup against Durham CCC (109 in 111 deliveries).

Mahmudul Hassan Joy century (Bangladesh)

Wonderful to see Bangladesh High Performance batsman Mahmudul Hassan Joy score 70 against New Zealand in the First Test. A very elegant and natural batsman.

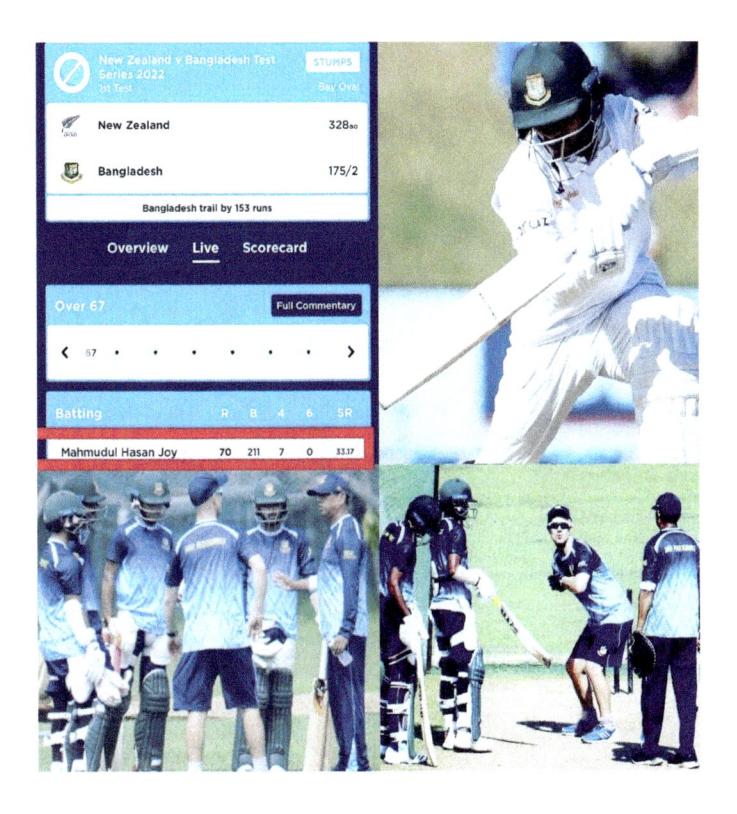

Jacques Banton (Worcestershire CCC)

Loved it when Jacques Banton had all his hard work rewarded with a contract at Worcestershire CCC.

Leon Johnson (Guyana)

Was very pleased when all of Leon Johnson's hard work was repaid with a century for Guyana against the Leeward Islands (102*)

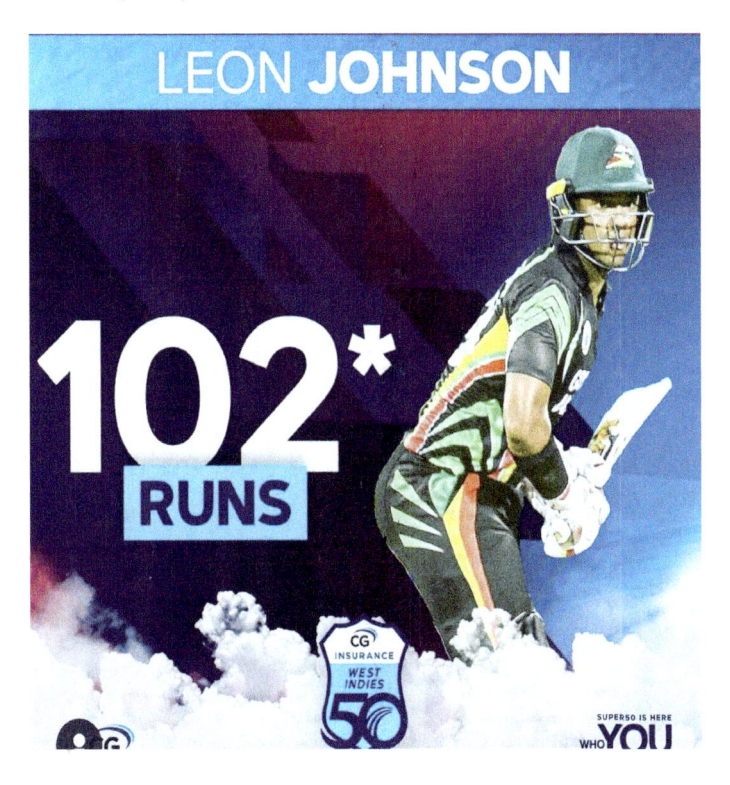

Saif Hassan (Bangladesh)

Saif Hassan hits a rich vein of form and blasts another century in the National Cricket League (Bangladesh)

Jonathan Carter (Barbados)

Jonathan Carter struck a wonderful century for Barbados in the 50-over Super Cup. Was chuffed for him!

Ajun Dal

Delighted to see that Ajun Dal has hit an unbeaten 114 for Derbyshire against Worcs today. An excellent batter, who works really hard to be even better. Enjoyed our coaching sessions when he came down to work with me in Cardiff.

Jacob Bethell

Congratulations to Jacob Bethell for his classy 61, on loan to Gloucestershire from Warwickshire, against Somerset in the championship. Jacob was one of our star batsmen, who helped the England Under-19s reach the World Cup final in March 2022, for the first time in 25 years. A top talent!

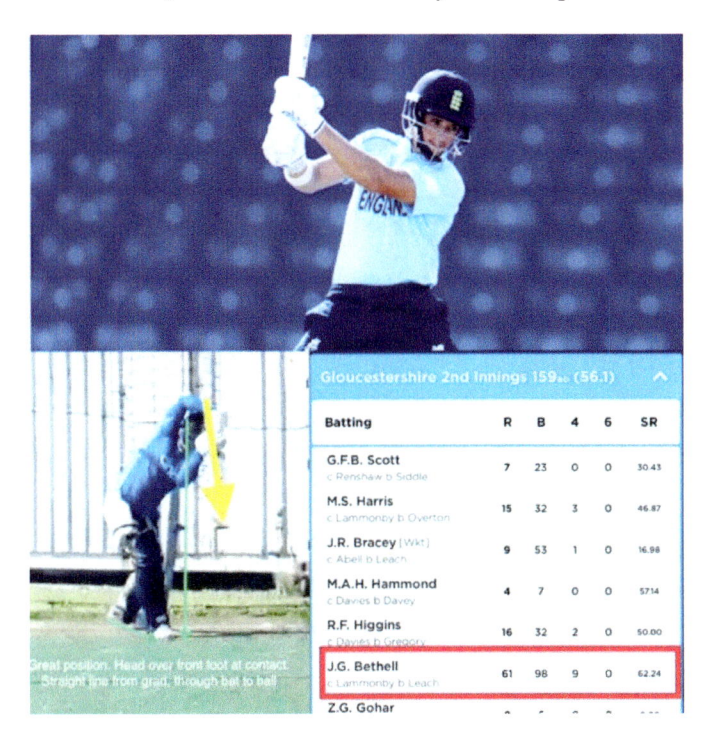

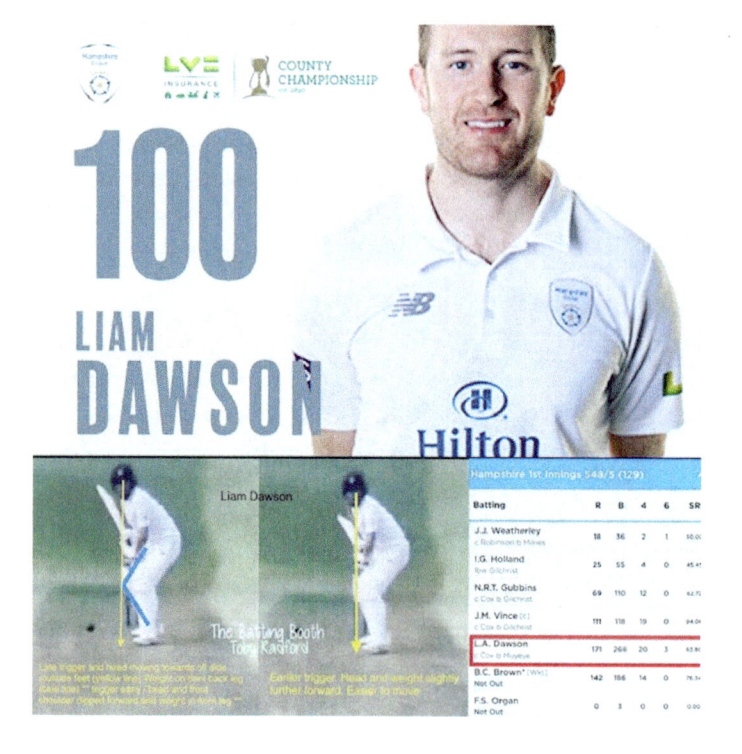

Liam Dawson

Liam Dawson struck a brilliant 171 for Hampshire against Kent, which included 20 fours and two sixes.

We had been working hard on Liam's balance at ball release. He also worked on an earlier trigger movement, with his head and weight slightly further forward to help with quicker movement, forward and back, and to access all lines of delivery.

Tom Prest (Hampshire CCC and England Young Lions)

England Young Lions captain Tom Prest worked extremely hard throughout the winter on his balance at ball release. He had a tendency for his head to fall slightly to the off side at ball release and to play across straighter deliveries.

He opened his front shoulder a fraction in his set-up and brought his head further forward towards the bowler's stumps.

By waiting longer at ball release and moving to the finishing line of the ball he was in a more balanced position at ball contact and able to present a fuller bat face at the ball.

I was delighted when he made 93 and 154 in back to back matches at the world cup – amassing 251 runs from just three group matches.

Photo courtesy of Getty Images
Tom Prest (England Young Lions captain and Hampshire CCC)

Daniel Bell-Drummond

Daniel Bell-Drummond struck back-to-back centuries for Kent after making changes to his set-up.

Left photo: Daniel has a lot of weight on his bent back leg, his hands and bat were a long way from his body (left hip), and the toe of his bat was almost behind his head.

With his hands so far outside off-stump at ball release, it was difficult for him to present a consistently straight bat path to the ball. I recommended a few changes.

Right photo: (following season) Dan is standing taller at the crease, with less weight on his back leg to enable quicker movement forward and back, and he's brought his hands and bat closer to his body (left hip) with the toe of the bat visible, and pointing towards first slip

With his hands closer to his body, and now inside the line of off-stump at ball release, it is easier for him to present a full bat face at all lines of delivery.

Other Photographs

Working With A World Cup Winner

Practising power hitting with West Indies World Cup winning batsman **Carlos Brathwaite**

Talking tactics with West Indies all-rounder **Roston Chase**

Ecstatic!

I almost jumped off the balcony when the West Indies beat England in a great Test Match at Headingley in 2017. Shai Hope scored centuries in both innings and Kraigg Brathwaite a century and a 90. It was a wonderful performance from the team.

Coach Education

I love working with coaches and I have written and delivered parts of the level 3 and level 4 coach education courses for ECB.

I have really enjoyed mentoring senior and advanced coaches for the ECB in recent years.

Talking Batting at the ECB Advanced batting module at Sussex CCC

Little and Large!

Relaxing with my good friend and world class West Indian all-rounder **Jason Holder**.

I first met Jason in 2010 when I set up the West Indies High Performance Centre in Barbados and Jason was at that first intake.

He was incredibly articulate and thoughtful and clearly a huge talent with both bat and ball.

We spent many hours on the bowling machine working on his batting and we have been great friends ever since. It's been a highlight of my career watching him develop into one of the finest all-rounders in the world. And he is still the same friendly and down-to-earth guy he always was.

I make sure that whenever he is in the UK he comes round to our house in Cardiff for one of my home-cooked steaks and a glass of red wine.

A top man!

Analysing batting footage from my home office in Cardiff

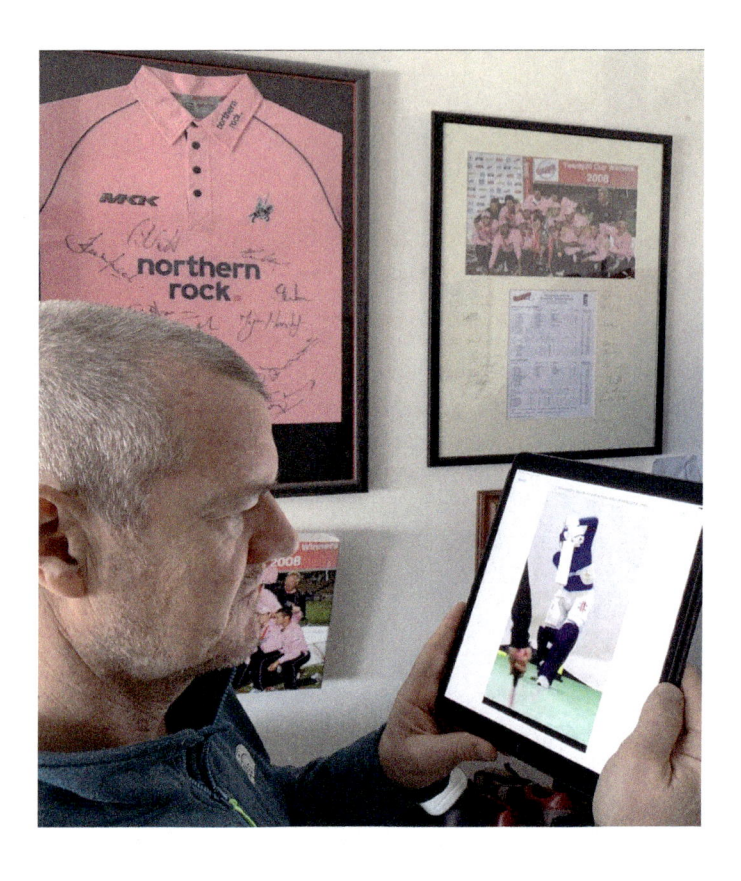

Enjoying a warm session in Dhaka with outstanding young batsman **Afif Dhrubo**

Discussing guard and pre-delivery movements with former West Indies legend **Dwayne Bravo**

The Coach's Eye

Watching on as Darren Bravo prepares for an upcoming One-Day series in Barbados

Making the most of a rain break

Taking every opportunity to work on a player's general performance at games in the indoor school during a rain-break at Queen's Park Oval, Trinidad

Modern Coaching!

Discussing batting with West Indian opener, Kieran Powell, via Zoom. From Cardiff to Leeward Islands. Magic!

Hitting Straight with West Indian superstar Kieron Pollard

Head should be in circle and shoulders on green and not red for around the wicket

Ackeem Auguste

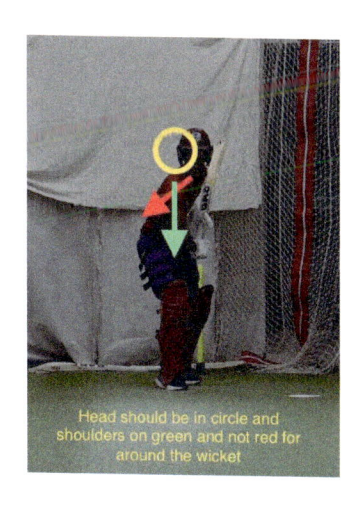

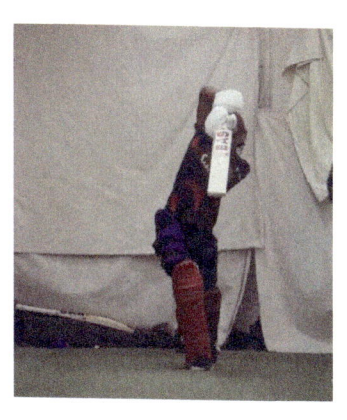

Ackeem Auguste, the West Indies under-19 world cup captain, spent 60 hours, over three weeks, with me in Cardiff, after flying over from the Leeward Islands.

We made subtle changes to his set-up, guard, weight distribution, and front hip position, to create a straighter bat path, quicker movement forward, and back, and tighter judgment of the ball around off-stump.

Coming Home

Touring is great, but there's nothing like getting back to see the family!

In Full Flight

Flinging off 16 yards to sharpen up West Indies before the first Test against England in Barbados in 2019

Feeling the Heat!

The temperature is close to 50 degrees centigrade in Abu Dhabi as the West Indies prepare to take on Pakistan. But the show must go on!

Family time

Enjoying a meal with Ayanna and Noah on the beautiful island of St Lucia

England Young Lions 2022

Photo courtesy of Getty images

I had a wonderful winter working as batting coach with the England Under 19s with head coach Richard Dawson and his wonderful support staff.

It was a highly talented and cohesive group of young players and we were all thrilled when they made it to England's first Under 19 World Cup final for 25 years, in Antigua in February 2022, falling just short to competition favourites, India.

Heading Up the Bangladesh High Performance Team

I have really enjoyed working with the incredibly dedicated and talented players as the head of High Performance for Bangladesh Cricket Board.

They soak up new information and have the ability to make subtle adjustments to their game very easily. They are a joy to work with.

I have loved watching Afif Dhrubo, Naim Sheikh and Mahmudul Hassan Joy, among others, who have progressed to, and performed well for the senior national team

BACK COVER:

Bangladesh nets
Babar Azam
Toby having a laugh in Abu Dhabi with West Indies
A club cricketer
England Women's captain Heather Knight

Printed in Great Britain
by Amazon